BLUEPRINTS
Science Investigations

Wendy and David Clemson

Second edition

Stanley Thornes (Publishers) Ltd

Do you receive BLUEPRINTS NEWS?

Blueprints is an expanding series of practical teacher's ideas books and photocopiable resources for use in primary schools. Books are available for separate infant and junior age ranges for every core and foundation subject, as well as for an ever widening range of other primary teaching needs. These include **Blueprints Primary English** books and **Blueprints Resource Banks**. Blueprints are carefully structured around the demands of the National Curriculum in England and Wales, but are used successfully by schools and teachers in Scotland, Northern Ireland and elsewhere.

Blueprints provide:
- *Total curriculum coverage*
- *Hundreds of practical ideas*
- *Books specifically for the age range you teach*
- *Flexible resources for the whole school or for individual teachers*
- *Excellent photocopiable sheets – ideal for assessment and children's work profiles*
- *Supreme value.*

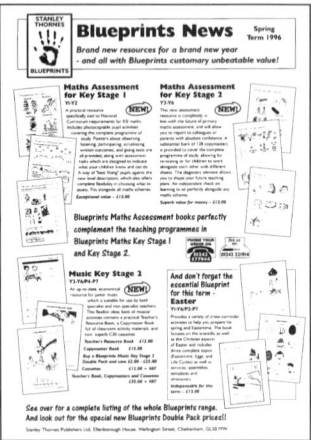

Books may be bought by credit card over the telephone and information obtained on **(01242) 577944**. Alternatively, photocopy and return this **FREEPOST** form to receive **Blueprints News**, our regular update on all new and existing titles. You may also like to add the name of a friend who would be interested in being on the mailing list.

Please add my name to the **BLUEPRINTS NEWS** mailing list.

Mr/Mrs/Miss/Ms _____

Home address _____

_____ Postcode _____

School address _____

_____ Postcode _____

Please also send **BLUEPRINTS NEWS** to:

Mr/Mrs/Miss/Ms _____

Address _____

_____ Postcode _____

To: Marketing Services Dept., Stanley Thornes Ltd, FREEPOST (GR 782), Cheltenham, GL50 1BR

© Text Wendy and David Clemson 1993
© Illustrations ST(P) Ltd 1993

The right of David and Wendy Clemson to be identified as authors of this work has been asserted by them in accordance with the Copyright, Designs and Patents Act 1988.

All rights reserved. No part of this publication may be reproduced or transmitted in any form or by any means, electronic or mechanical, including photocopy, recording or any information storage and retrieval system, without permission in writing from the publisher or under licence from the Copyright Licensing Agency Limited. Further details of such licences (for reprographic reproduction) may be obtained from the Copyright Licensing Agency Limited, of 90 Tottenham Court Road, London W1P 9HE.

Material from the National Curriculum is Crown copyright and is reproduced with the permission of the Controller of Her Majesty's Stationery Office.

The publishers have made every effort to contact copyright holders and will be only too pleased to acknowledge anyone overlooked.

First published in 1993 by:
Stanley Thornes (Publishers) Ltd
Ellenborough House
Wellington Street
CHELTENHAM GL50 1YW

Second edition 1995

A catalogue record for this book is available from the British Library.

ISBN 0 7487 2412 5

Typeset by Tech-Set, Gateshead, Tyne & Wear.
Printed and bound in Great Britain.

97 98 99 00 01 / 10 9 8 7 6 5 4 3 2

CONTENTS

Introduction   v

National Curriculum, Programme of study coverage summary chart   vi

Record sheet   viii

Teacher's notes on the copymasters   1–33

Copymasters 1–95

Section A: Levels 1/2
1. Extinct creatures
2. Sorting/classifying creatures
3. Fruit seed study
4. Healthy food for a day
5. Habitats for mini-beasts
6. Family likeness
7. Bread making
8. Texture and touch
9. Dyes
10. Play telephone
11. Seeing through
12. Secret writing
13. Mixing paints
14. Magnetic attraction
15. Mixing colours of light
16. Race around the park
17. Spinning snake
18. Teddy moves

Section B: Levels 3/4
19. Organic gardening and farming
20. Food chains
21. Nutritional value of cereals
22. Pet behaviour
23, 24. Pet care
25. Seed dispersal 1
26. Teeth
27. Trees
28. Camouflage
29. Hearing
30. Photography
31. Seed dispersal 2
32. Shoes
33. Building materials
34. Crystals
35. Drink in the desert
36. Filtering water
37. Swim fabrics
38. Tea making
39. Temperatures around school
40. Using light-sensitive paper

41. Reflective surfaces
42. Shadow playing
43. Balloon rocket
44. Colour filters
45. Cotton reel toy
46. Friction
47. Friction car and trailer
48. Good conductors
49. Make a stringed instrument
50. Mass and volume
51. Möbius band
52. Model theatre
53. Musical instruments
54. Noises and sound proofing
55. Optical illusions
56. Paddle boat
57. Paper aeroplanes
58. Poles of a magnet
59. Puck game
60. Pulleys
61. Sailing
62. Sand clock
63. See-saw
64. Signalling – Morse
65. Stopping force
66. Sundials
67. Using air pressure
68. Water clock
69. Weighing paper
70. Wheels

Section C: Level 5
71. Fingerprints
72. All-weather wear
73. Raindrops
74. Boats
75. Elasticity of springs
76. Electricity and magnetism
77. Hydraulics
78. Lock gates
79. Pelican crossing
80. Pendulum
81. Signalling – lighthouses
82. Skip
83. Spectrum
84. Speed and distance

Whole school investigations
85. Science in a rhyme
86. Bicycle
87. Conservation/pollution
88. Cooking
89. Play safe

Weekend science investigations
90 Bottle band
91 Shadows
92 Dissolving
93 Kaleidoscope
94 Periscope
95 Marble timer

Introduction

At the nub of scientific method is the idea of 'investigating', so much school science that children do could be called 'investigations'. Nevertheless, we felt we needed some ground rules for what to include in a book like this. We have settled for a definition of 'investigation' which includes the following:

- it should include things children can do independently of the teacher, at least to some extent
- it should, as far as is possible, not have one right answer
- it should lead children to think about what else they could do or find out using the same material, concepts or apparatus
- it should have some scientific purpose but may include work beyond science
- it may be related to 'real' problems of the everyday life sort but should also be fun to do for itself.

The investigations that are in this book are, quite intentionally a 'mixed bag'. Some are highly specific and some are so general that the children's first task will be to decide which part of the problem they will enquire into. Some are rooted in what scientists may see as basic concepts while others demand that children think and work beyond their initial understanding. There are three main sections to the book. Investigations 1–18 are for children at the start of their schooling. Investigations 19–70 are, in our opinion, predominantly for use with children in the middle years of their primary education. Investigations 71–84 are for children at the top end of the primary school. At the back of the book are some suggested *Whole school investigations* (85–90) which include some examples of the kind of work that could be taken on by a whole school or department, culminating in an exhibition, presentation to parents, or open day for pupils from other schools. Added to this are some sample investigations (91–95) that can be photocopied for children to do at home, with parental help. We have called these *Weekend science*.

Some copymasters are record sheets for children; some are to stimulate discussion and motivate children; and some are instruction sheets which help children to create things.

National Curriculum Coverage

Alongside the text for each investigation, you will find a reference to the part of the Programme of Study to which the investigation contributes. The investigations are arranged in three main sections. Section A investigations include work which is predominantly at Levels 1 and 2. Section B investigations correspond approximately to Levels 3 and 4, and Section C investigations broadly map on to Level 5. Section A investigations broadly map onto the Key Stage 1 Programme of Study. Those in other sections relate to the Key Stage 2 Programme of Study.

We have placed the investigations in each section according to the likely demands they make on the children, rather than in strict accordance with National Curriculum Levels. However, within each section those investigations which cover work assigned to Life processes and living things appear first, then those deemed to contribute to both Life processes and living things and Materials and their properties and/or Physical processes. Next come those which relate to Materials and their properties, those labelled Materials and their properties and Physical processes, and finally those that we consider part of work on Physical processes. A summary chart of how each investigation relates to these appears on pages vi–viii.

Key:

- Life processes and living things = LP&LT
- Materials and their properties = M&P
- Physical processes = PP

Experimental and investigative science
We have made no reference to Experimental and investigative science. The reason for this is that we believe investigative approaches to learning mean that children will do work which contributes to Experimental and investigative science in all the activities in this book.

How to use this book

The investigations in the book are numbered to correspond with the appropriate copymasters. Within the text for each investigation *The task in action* notes are to give you, the teacher, a picture of what the children should be doing and how the investigation should progress. *Teacher help and information* is intended to help you in offering support to the children and also in supplying additional or background information. *Connections and extensions* offer ways of joining the investigation to others in the book and suggest directions the children's work can take. There is a record sheet on page viii which enables you to record which investigations each child has tried.

Acknowledgements

Thank you to Brita Water Filter Systems Ltd and Ilford Ltd for their help and information.

National Curriculum Programme of Study coverage: summary chart

		LP&LT	M&P	PP
Section A: Levels 1/2				
1	Extinct creatures	•		
2	Sorting/classifying creatures	•		
3	Fruit seed study	•		
4	Healthy food for a day	•		
5	Habitats for mini-beasts	•		
6	Family likeness	•		
7	Bread making	•	•	
8	Texture and touch	•	•	
9	Dyes	•	•	
10	Play telephone	•		•
11	Seeing through	•		•
12	Secret writing		•	
13	Mixing paints		•	•
14	Magnetic attraction			•
15	Mixing colours of light			•
16	Race around the park			•
17	Spinning snake			•
18	Teddy moves			•
Section B: Levels 3/4				
19	Organic gardening and farming	•		
20	Food chains	•		
21	Nutritional value of cereals	•		
22	Pet behaviour	•		
23,24	Pet care	•		
25	Seed dispersal 1	•		
26	Teeth	•		
27	Trees	•		
28	Camouflage	•		
29	Hearing	•		•
30	Photography	•		•
31	Seed dispersal 2	•		•
32	Shoes	•	•	
33	Building materials		•	
34	Crystals		•	
35	Drink in the desert		•	
36	Filtering water		•	
37	Swim fabrics		•	
38	Tea making		•	
39	Temperatures around school		•	
40	Using light-sensitive paper		•	
41	Reflective surfaces			•
42	Shadow playing			•
43	Balloon rocket			•
44	Colour filters			•

	LP&LT	M&P	PP
Section B Cont.			
45 Cotton reel toy			•
46 Friction			•
47 Friction car and trailer			•
48 Good conductors			•
49 Make a stringed instrument			•
50 Mass and volume			•
51 Möbius band			•
52 Model theatre			•
53 Musical instruments			•
54 Noises and sound proofing			•
55 Optical illusions			•
56 Paddle boat			•
57 Paper aeroplanes			•
58 Poles of a magnet			•
59 Puck game			•
60 Pulleys			•
61 Sailing			•
62 Sand clock			•
63 See-saw			•
64 Signalling – Morse			•
65 Stopping force			•
66 Sundials			•
67 Using air pressure			•
68 Water clock			•
69 Weighing paper			•
70 Wheels			•
Section C: Level 5			
71 Fingerprints	•		
72 All-weather wear		•	
73 Raindrops		•	•
74 Boats		•	•
75 Elasticity of springs		•	•
76 Electricity and magnetism		•	•
77 Hydraulics			•
78 Lock gates			•
79 Pelican crossing			•
80 Pendulum			•
81 Signalling – lighthouses			•
82 Skip			•
83 Spectrum			•
84 Speed and distance			•
Whole school investigations			
85 Science in a rhyme	Children can work on all ATs depending on the experiments they devise.		
86 Bicycle			
87 Conservation/pollution			
88 Cooking			
89 Play safe			
Weekend science investigations			
90 Bottle band			•
91 Shadows			•
92 Dissolving		•	
93 Kaleidoscope			•
94 Periscope			•
95 Marble timer			•

Record sheet

Child's Name:
Tick the investigations tried

Teacher's Initials

Section A: Levels 1/2
1 Extinct creatures
2 Sorting/classifying creatures
3 Fruit seed study
4 Healthy food for a day
5 Habitats for mini-beasts
6 Family likeness
7 Bread making
8 Texture and touch
9 Dyes
10 Play telephone
11 Seeing through
12 Secret writing
13 Mixing paints
14 Magnetic attraction
15 Mixing colours of light
16 Race around the park
17 Spinning snake
18 Teddy moves

Section B: Levels 3/4
19 Organic gardening and farming
20 Food chains
21 Nutritional value of cereals
22 Pet behaviour
23, 24 Pet care
25 Seed dispersal 1
26 Teeth
27 Trees
28 Camouflage
29 Hearing
30 Photography
31 Seed dispersal 2
32 Shoes
33 Building materials
34 Crystals
35 Drink in the desert
36 Filtering water
37 Swim fabrics
38 Tea making
39 Temperatures around school
40 Using light-sensitive paper
41 Reflective surfaces
42 Shadow playing
43 Balloon rocket
44 Colour filters
45 Cotton reel toy
46 Friction
47 Friction car and trailer
48 Good conductors
49 Make a stringed instrument
50 Mass and volume
51 Möbius band
52 Model theatre
53 Musical instruments
54 Noises and sound proofing
55 Optical illusions
56 Paddle boat
57 Paper aeroplanes
58 Poles of a magnet
59 Puck game
60 Pulleys
61 Sailing
62 Sand clock
63 See-saw
64 Signalling – Morse
65 Stopping force
66 Sundials
67 Using air pressure
68 Water clock
69 Weighing paper
70 Wheels

Section C: Level 5
71 Fingerprints
72 All-weather wear
73 Raindrops
74 Boats
75 Elasticity of springs
76 Electricity and magnetism
77 Hydraulics
78 Lock gates
79 Pelican crossing
80 Pendulum
81 Signalling – lighthouses
82 Skip
83 Spectrum
84 Speed and distance

Whole school investigations
85 Science in a rhyme
86 Bicycle
87 Conservation/pollution
88 Cooking
89 Play safe

Weekend science investigations
90 Bottle band
91 Shadows
92 Dissolving
93 Kaleidoscope
94 Periscope
95 Marble timer

Section A: Levels 1/2

1: Extinct Creatures

Purpose
To find out about an extinct creature (dinosaurs in this case) and speculate about why it became extinct.

Resources
Books, pictures and information packs about dinosaurs and their demise.

The task in action
Using the copymaster as inspiration children are asked to conduct research into one dinosaur, and then discuss what may have caused its extinction.

Teacher help and information
The topic dinosaurs is not only of interest to many children, theories about their extinction can be found in the press and on television, and models are on display in a number of museums. To make this topic lively see if the children can get press information or visit a museum.

Connections and extensions
Ask the children to choose an animal that has become extinct more recently, and conduct similar research. Alternatively, let them find out about threatened species and the sources of the risks they face.

Link this work to whole school investigations 87: Conservation/pollution.

2: Sorting/classifying Creatures

Purpose
To give children the opportunity to look at some of the criteria used for grouping creatures.

Resources
Books about insects and other small creatures; a simple key to show how these are grouped; some real small creatures if they can be found around school.

The task in action
Using the pictures on the copymaster as starting points the children need to find out how we distinguish insects from other small creatures and what these other creatures might be called.

Teacher help and information
Good resourcing is important in making this classification investigation accessible to young children. If you cannot find a good simple key, draw one yourself that the children can use. For example, if you wish the children to establish that an insect is a living creature with six legs, they need to apply some of the criteria for 'living' (that is feeds, moves etc.) and then ask the question 'Does it have six legs?' If small creatures are collected from the school grounds they should not be exposed to extremes of heat, light or vibration and should be returned as quickly as possible to the habitat they came from.

Connections and extensions
Connect this work to all other investigations about the living world, so that children have the chance to see that all creatures and plants are placed in groups, according to how they look and how they behave. Examples include investigations 5: Habitats for mini-beasts and 26: Teeth.

3: Fruit Seed Study

Purpose
To find the patterns and numbers of seeds in a variety of fruits and to begin to understand the chain seed–plant –seed.

Resources
A variety of fresh fruits in season; a sharp knife; compost and growing containers.

The task in action
Ask the children to try to predict the numbers of seeds in, for example, an apple, and the arrangement of these. Cut open the apple (if possible, cut several in a number of different directions through a part of the core). Let the children draw some of the patterns they see. Try the same procedure with other fruits. Let the children plant some of the seeds to see if any grow and discuss what they will grow into.

Teacher help and information
Avoid fruits with too many or inconspicuous pips. Cherries and grapes appear on the copymaster, along

with apple, pear and orange because they are commonly available, but other fruits like avocado or peach sometimes grow well in the correct conditions. Non-edible fruits like acorns, beech nuts and conkers could be useful too.

Connections and extensions
Link to investigations 25: Seed dispersal 1 and 31: Seed dispersal 2.

4: Healthy Food for a Day

Purpose
To introduce the idea that we need to eat a variety of foods to stay healthy.

Resources
A variety of real foods, play foods or food packaging; drawing materials and scissors; paper plates.

The task in action
The children are asked to find and draw the foods in three healthy meals.

Teacher help and information
Let the children identify and talk about real foods or handle, play with and talk about play foods. Let them draw and cut out sample foods or paint some on stiff card for them to use. You can then re-use these with other sets of children. Let the children choose and arrange foods on some paper plates, to make typical meals. Talk to them about the main food groups (carbohydrates, proteins, fats, vitamins and minerals) and where these appear in foods.

Pudding plates have been left off the copymaster. If you wish to discuss puddings with the children, then let them use a second copy of the copymaster. The plates could be cut from each child's copymaster and added to 'healthy breakfast' sets and so on.

Connections and extensions
Link a diet which is healthy for humans with discussions of what might prove healthy for other animals including pets. Link also to investigations 21: Nutritional value of cereals and 23,24: Pet care.

5: Habitats for Mini-beasts

Purpose
To create and explore a mini-beast habitat.

Resources
Damp places in the school grounds that are relatively undisturbed; large stones that can be lifted; books about insects and other small creatures.

The task in action
The copymaster tells the children to draw what they find under a stone they have deliberately set down in a suitable environment to form a mini-beast habitat.

Teacher help and information
Ten days may not be long enough to encourage small creatures to adopt the habitat. If this is the case, try to ensure that the stone is undisturbed and carefully lift it every ten days. If it remains still and is damp it will eventually attract beetles, ants, woodlice, snails, worms, millipedes and the like.

Connections and extensions
Let the children try anchoring a piece of sheet plastic over rough grass. The grass will die and small creatures will be attracted to the rotting vegetation. Arrange a number of stones in a variety of locations so that the children can see which locations the creatures prefer.

Links can be made to investigation 2: Sorting/classifying creatures.

6: Family Likeness

Purpose
To talk about likenesses and differences within a species, in this case humans.

Resources
Family photographs (with names on the back) which the children can bring into school.

The task in action
The children look for and talk about family likenesses and draw pictures of the faces of their grandparents, their parents and themselves.

Teacher help and information
This investigation requires sensitive introduction. Some children may be in a one-parent family, be adopted or in care, or they may never have known their dead or distant parents or grandparents.

Connections and extensions
Link this work to investigations involving differences within species, like investigation 71: Fingerprints, and between species, like investigations 2: Sorting/classifying creatures and 26: Teeth.

7: Bread Making

Purpose
To make a record of an experiment using the senses and to observe the permanent changes caused by using yeast and heat with the other ingredients in bread making.

Resources
A bread recipe and the appropriate ingredients (if you use dried yeast you may find a suitable recipe on the sachet); aprons and oven gloves; cooking utensils; loaf tins and an oven.

The task in action
The children should be able to talk about what is happening and what their senses are telling them throughout the bread making experiment, and use the copymaster to record some of the sensations. A follow-up discussion can help the children understand what their senses are and the kind of information each one supplies, and the idea that things sometimes change when they are mixed together and heated.

Teacher help and information
This investigation is to be a combination of sensing, talking and recording. Give the children opportunities, every ten minutes, to record what their senses tell them. They will have seen what happens to the mixture when the yeast is added. When they are eating the bread they will understand, with your help, that the change from dough to bread is permanent.

Connections and extensions
Link this to investigation 12: Secret writing.

8: Texture and Touch

Purpose
To explore the sense of touch through the texture of materials and texture vocabulary.

Resources
A vast quantity of fabric samples, and samples of other materials suitable for collage work, for example, sand, corrugated card, moulded packaging, petals, leaves, feathers, netting; PVA glue; stout background paper or card; scissors.

The task in action
By choosing, cutting, gluing and sticking the children are required to make a 'feely' picture for a mole (because moles have very poor eyesight).

Teacher help and information
The 'feely' picture is a vehicle for the start of a discussion about our sense of touch and the characteristics of different materials. Thus the talk is actually more important than the task and should yield a vocabulary list for classroom display.

Connections and extensions
You may wish to extend the children's work by taking up some of their discussion points. For example, if a child says 'This bit of silk is slippery and this other bit of material isn't', you could ask him or her about the uses of different fabrics, how we test a fabric for slipperiness, when we do not want it to slip etc. The discussion could extend to the important characteristics of other materials. For example, 'the houses belonging to the three little pigs' could be a starting point for enquiries into building materials and their suitability in various situations.

9: Dyes

Purpose
To explore ways in which dyes might be made from natural materials and to investigate which dyes work best with different fabrics.

Resources
A range of plant and food material such as onions, raspberries, carrots, tomatoes, tea, coffee and elderberries; a range of pieces of fabric of different kinds; water and containers.

The task in action
Using whatever materials the children wish they should attempt to make dyes to try on different fabrics. They should test how their dyes bear up to exposure to sunlight and washing.

Teacher help and information
It is only comparatively recently that dyes have been produced through the chemical industry. For centuries dyes were obtained from plant materials. The dye solution can be made by boiling. For example, good results can be obtained with onion skins if you boil them up until the 'onion water' is a good strong colour. Allow the pan to cool, strain off the skins and soak the fabrics in the remaining liquid for a few hours. After a quick rinse they can be hung up to dry.

Connections and extensions
Try tie-dyeing. A button or coin can be trapped within an elastic band on a piece of fabric. The little pouch containing the button or coin can be dipped in the dye and when dried off a circular pattern emerges. Paper can also be tie-dyed effectively, when folded in a variety

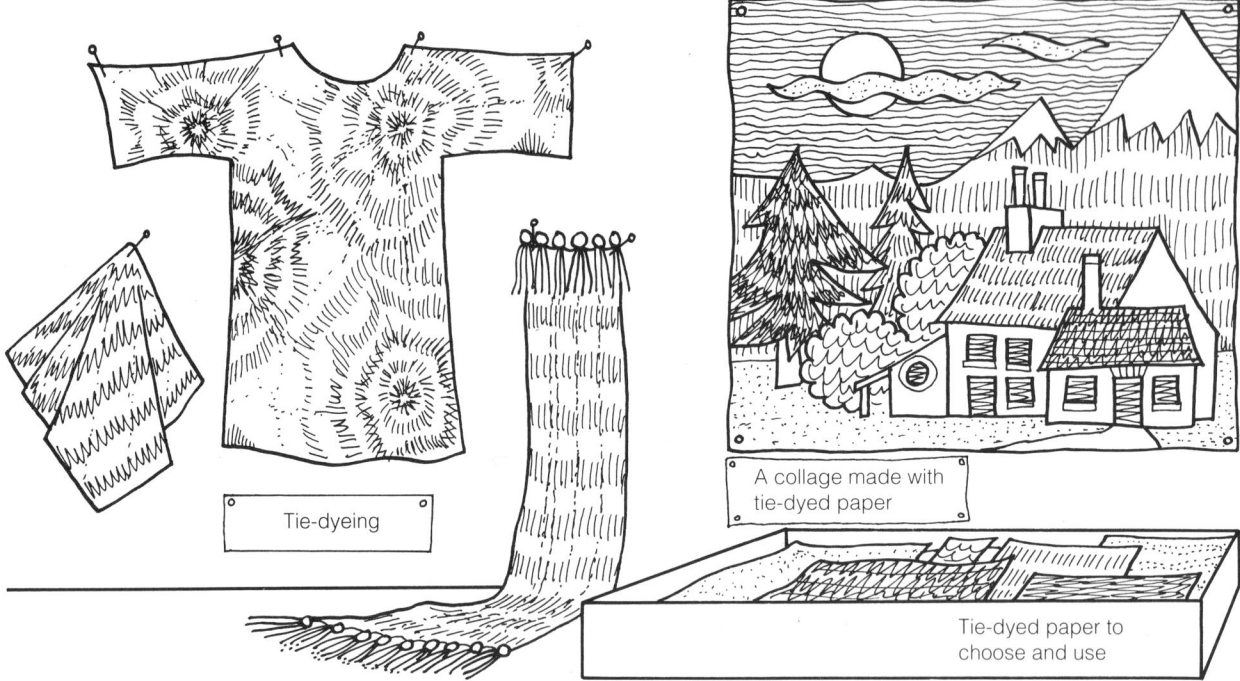

Tie-dyeing

A collage made with tie-dyed paper

Tie-dyed paper to choose and use

of ways. This makes very innovative collage material. The children can also explore the use of dyes in other cultures and at different times in history.

Compare dye making with the mixing of pigments in art work; see investigation 13: Mixing paints.

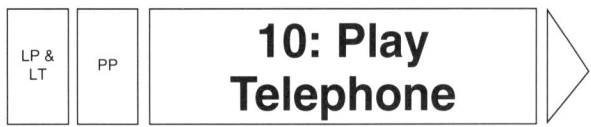

10: Play Telephone

Purpose
To learn that a special movement, called vibration, is necessary to produce and transmit sound.

Resources
Empty cocoa tins, or other tins without a jagged edge; string, hammer and nails, buttons; funnels, plastic tubing, blown-up balloon.

The task in action
Having made a play telephone to match one of the pictures on the copymaster, the child is asked to establish whether the string needs to be taut and whether, using a balloon, sounds can be felt as well as heard.

Teacher help and information
Remind the children that they need to whisper. With not too long a string they are tempted to shout, and then do not need the telephone! The string or hose does need to be taut to enable the sound to travel well.

Connections and extensions
Extend what the children do by getting them to see what happens when they vary the size of the cans or the length of the string, and see if they can feel the sounds through their chests, chins or other parts of the body.

Link this work to investigation 54: Noises and sound proofing.

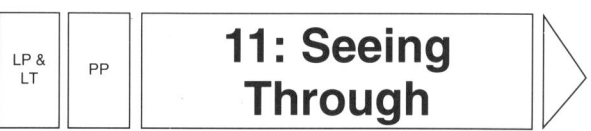

11: Seeing Through

Purpose
To sort and identify materials that are transparent, translucent and opaque, and to understand that light therefore passes through some materials and not others.

Resources
A wide variety of materials and lists of materials found around the school, in, for example, buildings, equipment and resources.

The task in action
The children can write about or draw a variety of materials which fit one of three sets:

- completely see through
- partly see through
- not see through.

Teacher help and information
As well as small samples of, for example, translucent plastic, wood, and paper, encourage the children to try looking through windows, walls, the blackboard, a book, a cushion, and a fizzy drink.

Connections and extensions
Connect this investigation to others about light including investigation 42: Shadow playing and weekend science investigations 93: Kaleidoscope and 94: Periscope.

12: Secret Writing

Purpose
To understand that some materials change when heated and that the change is permanent.

Resources
Lemons and lemon squeezer; fine paint brushes, paper; electric oven on at a low temperature.

The task in action
Each child writes an 'invisible' message with a paint brush dipped in lemon juice. When the paper is dry you should place it in a low oven, where the lemon juice will turn brown, revealing the message.

Teacher help and information
Using the copymaster as a starting point to the discussion, let the children complete their messages. Keeping the children at a safe distance from the oven, let them observe what has happened when you take the paper out of the oven. Ask them whether they think their messages will become invisible again (perhaps when they are cool). The lemon juice undergoes a permanent chemical change when heated and the change cannot be reversed.

Connections and extensions
Extend this work by talking about and experimenting with other materials that change when heated. Examples of *temporary* changes occur with table jelly and chocolate, and *permanent* changes occur in modelling clay, eggs, cake mix and bread dough. Connect this to investigation 7: Bread making and whole school investigation 88: Cooking.

13: Mixing Paints

Purpose
To experiment with mixing paint pigments.

Resources
Overalls; paints, paper, brushes; lots of pots of water and cloths for brush cleaning; mixing palettes (old plates or saucers will do).

The task in action
The children can try mixing the paints to make new colours. If you let them paint a pattern with their colours they can later attach their colour mix card to it for the display.

Teacher help and information
The important point for the children, apart from a knowledge of which colours to mix in future painting, is that mixing pigments changes them. Colours of light, when mixed, do not produce the same results. For example, red light mixed with green light produces yellow light.

Connections and extensions
Many of the colours in everyday use are made by mixing dyes. Felt-tip pen ink and sugar-coated chocolate buttons produce a band of colours when put onto damp blotting paper.

Link this work to investigations 9: Dyes and 15: Mixing colours of light.

Mixing colours of paint

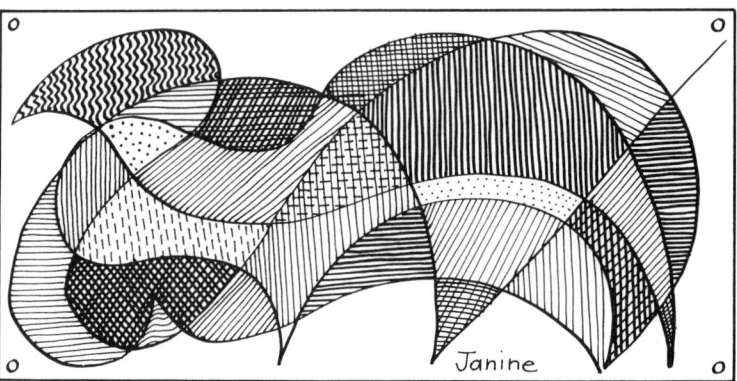

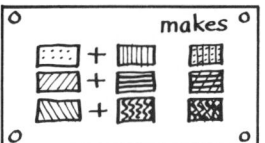

Here are some of the colours Yoseph mixed

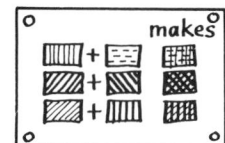

Can you see Janine's mixed colours in her picture?

14: Magnetic Attraction

Purpose
To find out what kinds of things are attracted by a magnet and what materials magnets can work through.

Resources
Magnets; a wide variety of small items, including those that appear on the copymaster, to test the magnet on; materials, as listed on the copymaster, through which to test the magnet.

The task in action
The children are asked to tick whether any of a number of things shown on the copymaster are attracted by a magnet, and then to find out if the magnet works through a variety of materials.

Teacher help and information
Children should be able to conduct this investigation with little help. Discuss their conclusions. Things with iron and steel in them are attracted by a magnet. Depending on the strength of the magnet and the thickness of the material, magnets can work through all the materials listed on the copymaster.

Connections and extensions
Link this work to investigation 16: Race around the park.

15: Mixing Colours of Light

Purpose
To see what happens when colours of light mix.

Resources
Coloured pencils or felt-tip pens; scissors; thin card; a knitting needle or something similar to make holes in the spinners; thread and spent matchsticks.

The task in action
The children can colour the spinners, using their own choice of colours, in any way they wish. They then make thread or matchstick spinners and look at the changing colour effects as the spinners are rotated.

Teacher help and information
Light mixes do not work in the same way as pigment mixes. We see 'blue' card as blue because all the other colours of light going to make up white light are absorbed and the blue light is reflected into our eyes. If we could mix all rainbow light colours we should see white light.

Connections and extensions
Link this work to investigation 44: Colour filters.

16: Race Around the Park

Purpose
To make a game using magnets and their properties of attraction.

Resources
Two small magnets; stiff card; drinking straws or pipe cleaners; scissors; felt-tip pens; paper clips.

The task in action
The children can colour in the game board on the copymaster and cut out the play strips. Having strengthened the play strips if necessary, they can stick

magnets on the ends and colour and glue the play pieces ready for the game.

Teacher help and information
The copymaster should be copied onto thin card or copied and then stuck on card. The play strips may still need reinforcement using card, straws or pipe cleaners. The play board needs to be set between two tables or above a table surface so that the children can get their hands under the board.

Connections and extensions
Link this work to investigation 14: Magnetic attraction.

17: Spinning Snake

Purpose
To demonstrate that warm air rises.

Resources
Scissors; felt-tip pens; copymaster photocopied onto thin card or glued to thin card; thread; sticky tape.

The task in action
Let the children colour and cut out the snake shape on the copymaster.

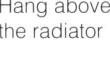
Hang above the radiator

Teacher help and information
Thread the shapes onto cotton and attach them above a radiator.

Connections and extensions
Link this work to investigation 39: Temperatures around school.

18: Teddy Moves

Purpose
Try to create forces that will move a toy, independent of human push or pull.

Resources
As this investigation is completely open the required resources will depend on what the children decide to do, but will probably include junk materials.

The task in action
The children have to move a teddy across the room without human power.

Teacher help and information
Let the children work in pairs if this is appropriate. They can plan what they are going to try and then have a design meeting with you to establish that they have all the resources they need and that what they are planning is not dangerous. If they are stuck for ideas you could suggest they use gravity or a vehicle powered by a wound elastic band.

Connections and extensions
Depending on the sophistication of the inventions you can offer the children new challenges, including, for example, can teddy be made to climb a hill? Can you make teddy move slower or faster? Would it be easier to move a lighter toy?

This investigation can be linked to others concerned with forces and movement, for example, 45: Cotton reel toy.

Section B: Levels 3/4

19: Organic Gardening and Farming

Purpose
To find out what organic gardening and farming is and to try to determine whether organically produced vegetables look and taste different from others.

Resources
Reference books about organic gardening and farming; organic vegetables and similar non-organic ones.

The task in action
The children have to find out about organic gardening and record what it is, and find out whether they themselves and a sample of ten other people prefer organic vegetables and if so why.

Teacher help and information
If possible, give the children the chance to go shopping for the vegetables. They can then discuss the relative importance the shops give to organic and non-organic produce, by noting their locations in the shops, how they are priced and the volumes of stocks kept.

Connections and extensions
Let the children conduct some more work into the kinds of fertilisers in use and how these affect yields, what a food 'mountain' is and why these occur, and other topical issues raised in the press about the food we eat.
   Link this work to investigations 4: Healthy food for a day and 21: Nutritional value of cereals.

20: Food Chains

Purpose
To find out about food chains and the importance of plants in these chains.

Resources
Reference books about the animal kingdom, dietary habits of animals and plant names.

The task in action
The children have to find and draw some food chains.

Teacher help and information
When their enquiries have been wide-ranging, the children should be able to make general statements about chains. Help them to come to understand that all food chains depend, ultimately, on plants and that all the creatures in a chain are interdependent. If one species dies or becomes extinct all the others are at risk.

Connections and extensions
The idea of chains of natural events can be developed by linking this work to investigations 3: Fruit seed study and 25: Seed dispersal 1.

21: Nutritional Value of Cereals

Purpose
To examine which of a range of breakfast cereals might contribute most to a healthy diet.

Resources
Six different cereal packets; books and information about healthy diets for children.

The task in action
Let the children look at the nutritional information panels on the cereal packs to determine the yield of each in calories, protein, sugar, fibre and two other ingredients of their choice. They need to rank the cereals on each nutritional component.

Teacher help and information
Before the children begin this investigation they will need to be 'primed' about what is a good diet, and shown that in interpreting the rankings they will not necessarily be looking at what comes top each time. For example, the cereal that has least sugar but most protein might be regarded as being the most nutritious.

Connections and extensions
The investigation does ignore two crucial factors in cereal choice - taste and consistency. Extend the children's work by letting them choose other criteria for measuring 'cereal acceptability'. Ask them to investigate and compare other food products, for example, biscuits, baked beans, bread or tinned fish.
   Link this work to investigation 4: Healthy food for a day.

22: Pet Behaviour

Purpose
To explore a variety of behaviours in pets and compile an information file based on observations.

Resources
A variety of pets, which may include, for example, fish, reptiles, mammals and birds; or perhaps a variety of mammals, for example, cats, dogs, rabbits, gerbils and mice. (Unless these animals are available in school, this investigation can only be done by children at home, using their own pets.)

The task in action
Give the children the copymaster on which to make notes. Let them record as many behaviours as they can over a period of about two weeks.

Teacher help and information
When children bring their notes into school discuss ways of presenting the results so that other children can read them. Discuss possible interpretations for behaviours, for example, the dog's wagging tail means (to humans) that he is pleased. Help the children collate their results to make a dossier or display.

Connections and extensions
Put the information compiled onto an animal behaviour database.
Link this work to investigation 23,24: Pet care.

Connections and extensions
Tie this work into more general discussions about the need to care for all animals using, for example, the whole school investigation 87: Conservation/pollution.
Link this work to investigation 22: Pet behaviour.

 23, 24: Pet Care

Purpose
To learn about the care of living things and some of the essentials necessary to animal health.

Resources
Books and information about pet care; information from organisations like the RSPCA and RSPB or pet experts like the proprietor of a cattery or a local vet; a list of pets belonging to children in the class. If there are no pets in school, if only for the sake of children who do not have a pet of their own that they could study, arrange for someone to bring in a pet for a day. Be sure to arrange adequate accommodation for visiting pets and observe the official rules and regulations regarding their safety and that of the children.

The task in action
The two copymasters are the pages of a little booklet that each child can create about a pet of his or her choice. One page of the booklet has been left blank so that each child can choose an additional aspect.

Teacher help and information
Each copymaster has two double pages on it and these can be stapled or sewn together to form the book.

25: Seed Dispersal 1

Purpose
To learn about the dispersal of seeds by birds.

Resources
Bird table; variety of fruits, including, for example, blackberries, elderberries, hawthorn berries and other non-poisonous fruits; flower pots and growing medium.

The task in action
The children are asked to plant bird droppings, once they have tempted the birds to eat a variety of fruits. If successful, seedlings will grow from the planted bird droppings.

Teacher help and information
Scraping up droppings may not appeal to some children. Remind them of health and safety rules and let them wear rubber gloves when scraping up. This work can be done over quite a long period, using different fruits as they come into season. Check that the children know which fruits to avoid as some can be poisonous. Clearly, any plants that grow from the bird droppings may not be of the type of fruit used to lure the birds to the table. However, the children should come to understand that seeds can survive in passing through birds and that the seeds from the fruit will be transported elsewhere by the birds.

Connections and extensions
To extend this work the children could discuss how they can improve on their experiment. For example, if you have different species of fruit-eating birds around the school, the children could observe which fruits the species seem to prefer. Two bird tables with different fruits may attract different species and produce species-matched droppings for planting.
Link this work to investigations 3: Fruit seed study and 31: Seed dispersal 2.

| LP & LT | **26: Teeth** ▷ |

Purpose
To study the dentition of several animals as a guide to similarities and differences between species.

Resources
Books on animals which describe their diets and lifestyle; a computer and database package; if possible a range of skulls of different animals.

The task in action
The children have to examine pictures and, if possible, real animal teeth in order to suggest ways in which the teeth are similar and different. Using their initial explorations they should then look at books and pictures in order to assemble a list of different animals with different configurations of teeth. The list can be used to construct a database.

Teacher help and information
The extent of this investigation will depend on the resources you can provide. Some of the key concepts are indicated below.

Connections and extensions
Extend the work by looking at some other part of an animal's skeleton or lifestyle and studying differences between it and other animals. Examples could include feet, care of the young, homes and habitats.

Link this work to investigation 2: Sorting/classifying creatures.

| LP & LT | **27: Trees** ▷ |

Purpose
To find out why trees are the shapes they are and what purpose leaves serve, and so learn how trees get the nutrients they require.

Resources
A variety of trees in the school grounds, gardens or park; books about trees and photosynthesis.

The task in action
The children are asked to draw some trees and then try to determine some possible answers to a number of questions about leaves. Using their findings they are then asked to design and make a model tree.

Teacher help and information
After they have made their observations the children should have the opportunity to research their enquiries through the school library and the library service. You should encourage the development of a resource bank of information and ideas sharing amongst the children. From their enquiries you should expect information such as:

- leaves contain chlorophyll for photosynthesis
- leaf canopies spread to allow the maximum light to hit all leaves
- deciduous trees shed their leaves in the autumn
- different sorts of tree seem to prefer different habitats.

Teeth are used for:

Herbivore
 Cutting
 Grinding

Carnivore
 Tearing
 Crushing

Omnivore
 All these actions

10

Connections and extensions
This work can support a range of environmental projects as well as work on animal habitats and the forestry industry.
Link this work to investigation 30: Photography.

28: Camouflage

Purpose
To find out what we mean by camouflage and how it is useful in the animal world. To look for instances where people deliberately make things stand out from a background and to explain how this is achieved.

Resources
Reference books, magazines, postcard pictures and brochures about the animal kingdom; wildlife videos and slides; sugar paper, card, staples, pins, scissors, felt-tip pens and other art materials.

The task in action
The copymaster comprises two headings for a display that can come out of work on camouflage. The children need to find out all they can about camouflage in the animal kingdom using secondary sources and to assemble explanations, pictures and reasons for camouflage on a display. Alongside this they can set a number of examples of things standing out from their backgrounds. They can record explanations as to how this is achieved and circumstances in which distinct images may be important.

Teacher help and information
This is an investigation that is wide-ranging with many possible lines of development. Help the children to research not only larger animals and birds but also creatures like moths. Discussions can extend into the need for camouflage by soldiers, hunters and bird watchers. Colours that stand away from their backgrounds are used extensively in, for example, advertising, road signs, art and fashion.

Connections and extensions
Let the children devise an experiment to test which colours blend best with, say, a town or countryside environment, and which colour combinations are most eye catching. They can set up some experimental viewing cards and let a sample of children see and rate them.
Link this work to whole school investigation 87: Conservation/pollution.

29: Hearing

Purpose
To find out about the acuity of our hearing.

Resources
Surveyor's spool measuring tape; trundle wheel; things to make sounds including, for example, paper clips, tin lid, wooden blocks, maracas.

The task in action
The picture on the copymaster should give the children a clue about how to set up an experiment to test each other's hearing.

Teacher help and information
This is an investigation which may need sensitive handling as there may be children with impaired hearing in the class.

Connections and extensions
Extended work can be provided by issuing the children with challenges, for example:
Do we hear better indoors?
Does the direction of the wind affect our hearing?
Can we hear better with our eyes shut?
Can we hear better with both ears? (Try an ear muff on one ear.)
Link this work to other sense investigations including 7: Bread making and 8: Texture and touch.

 30: Photography

Purpose
To help children understand how a camera works and have practice in taking photographs.

Resources
Cameras and film.

The task in action
Having looked carefully at a camera the children are asked to identify its main parts, talk about and draw what happens inside it, and finally take some photographs.

Teacher help and information
Make sure the children know what the main parts of the camera are and what they are for. Open an empty camera and show them where the film goes. Tell the children that a loaded camera must not be opened, until all the film is used and wound back. Remind the children about the care of cameras, including, for example, using the safety strap and not touching the lens. Try to give the children the opportunity to use the camera as a recording device for environmental change, and to demonstrate the bias of the viewer and the partial information given by a photograph. For example, photographs could yield the pattern of shadow cast by a tree in a day, but they can present ambiguities in direction (which way up?) and in timing.

Connections and extensions
Link this work to investigations 27: Trees and 40: Using light-sensitive paper.

The photographs taken could be starting points for discussion about the working of the human eye, what we mean by 'eye level' and the different kinds of information we get from a still, in contrast to a moving, image.

Purpose
To learn about the ways in which seeds are dispersed, to collect tree fruits that are 'winged' and test their flight.

Resources
Tree fruits; books about trees.

The task in action
The children are invited to find out about seed dispersal and identify the fruits of some trees and how they are spread. They should then collect some fruits and test how each of them flies.

Teacher help and information
This is an investigation for late September to November when tree fruits are ripe. Help the children to be systematic in their experimentation and the recording of results. They could tabulate results or, if you have enough sample fruits, they could be stuck onto the children's record sheets in the appropriate places.

Connections and extensions
Link this work to investigations 3: Fruit seed study, 25: Seed dispersal 1 and 57: Paper aeroplanes.

Purpose
To investigate the decisions that are made when producing things suitable for a large number of people who are all different, and to look at some of the properties of materials.

Resources
Information from shoe manufacturers about the sizes and fittings they supply; a foot size chart; a list of materials commonly used in shoe manufacture.

The task in action
The copymaster presents a list of kinds of information the children need to collect. The copymaster is also intended to form the cover or first page of a book or folder about the children's data collection and findings.

Teacher help and information
Help the children systematise their information collection by setting down the details in tabular form.

Connections and extensions
Link this work to investigations 37: Swim fabrics, 46: Friction and 72: All-weather wear.

Purpose
To find out which building materials are in common use and why they are used.

Resources
Access to a main street and the materials of which the buildings are constructed; samples of building materials with name labels; information about building materials and some of the reasons why they are used.

The task in action
Let the children, with plenty of adult supervision, walk along a main street, making a drawing of some of the buildings that appear in a section of it. They then have to find out what materials are used in the buildings, where the materials came from and why they may have been chosen.

Teacher help and information
Talk to the children before they begin this investigation, and show them the building material samples. Explain what they are called. Give the children a wide range of background information, for example, some children may not know how concrete is made or what breeze blocks are, they may not have handled slate or know that window frames nowadays are sometimes plastic. Walk along the main street by yourself before you take the children and find out what the materials are. You can then become the expert and answer all the children's questions.

Connections and extensions
Link this work to investigation 30: Photography, using this as one method of recording the architecture of the local community.

34: Crystals

Purpose
To grow a crystal and examine its characteristics and the length of time it takes to grow.

Resources
Sugar, salt, water, a spoon, pipe cleaners; other objects for suspension; string or thread; a clear plastic or glass container.

The task in action
Make a strong sugar solution in a clear plastic or glass container and suspend a spoon in it, using string or thread, or just insert a pipe-cleaner or thread in the solution. Observations should be made periodically to see what is happening. Drawings should be made after one, two and three weeks. Try the same experiment with a salt solution, starting the salt a week after the sugar.

Teacher help and information
Show the children that sugar fails to dissolve when the solution is *saturated*. This means that no more sugar is capable of being dissolved and any added will just lie at the base of the container. It often helps to 'seed' the crystal growth and this can be achieved, for example, by dipping thread in a little glue and then into sugar before suspending it in the saturated solution. In recent years there has been a growth in the sale of cheap crystal-growing kits – some of the children may have these at home and might be able to share them with the class.

Connections and extensions
Let the children look at the crystals under strong magnifiers and draw what they see.

Visit a geological museum or borrow some rock crystals, for the children to look at. See if the children can make models of the rock crystals they have seen using construction straws. This can be linked to three-dimensional shapes work in mathematics.

35: Drink in the Desert

Purpose
To show that water evaporates into the air and that some of the water vapour from the air can be recondensed.

Resources
Flowerpot, short bean stick, clear plastic sheeting; washing-up bowl, tray larger than bowl; water.

The task in action
Having tried the experiment set out on the copymaster, the children are required to modify this experiment in order to surmise that they could get a drink in the desert. In the classroom experiment the children should find that water condenses in droplets on the underside of the sheeting and eventually runs down to the edge of the bowl where it could be collected.

Teacher help and information
The copymaster experiment is similar to a simple form of 'still' like that used in the manufacture of spirits. The desert traveller has to make sure of catching every drop of water to quench the thirst, for once it falls on the sand the process of evaporation and condensation begins again. It is necessary also to dig a bowl shaped hole in which to set the stick.

Connections and extensions
Link this to work on the weather.

36: Filtering Water

Purpose
To explore the idea of filtration and the reasons why the process is important to us in our everyday lives.

Resources
A water filter jug; watch or clock; a range of materials including sand, gravel, pebbles, coffee filters; containers and supports; plenty of water.

The task in action
The children should try out a water filter jug having examined its parts and seen how they are put together. They can try timing how long it takes for different quantities of water to be filtered. They should discuss why some people feel the need to make use of water filter jugs. Using the pebbles, gravel and sand they should then attempt to make a filter pouring muddy water in at the top and examining it for colour at the bottom. They should attempt this using each material alone and then try stacking them, for example, sand covered by gravel covered by pebbles. How long does it take to filter a given quantity of water? Comparisons can then be made with the filtering capability of a coffee filter. Would paper be robust enough? How many times can the coffee filter be used? The copymaster should be used for reporting the experiment.

Teacher help and information
Commercially-produced water filters commonly use a cartridge containing food grade resin and vegetable carbon which is especially treated so that it retains substances like those that cause temporary water 'hardness', chlorine and its compounds, and lead and copper. The filter the children produce will only be capable of demonstrating the principle of filtration and on no account should their filtered water be drunk.

Connections and extensions
Let the children try taste tests on tap water and water that has been filtered through the jug. Find out from water authorities what is done to purify our tap water and how sewage is treated. Study the water cycle.

Link this work to whole school investigation 87: Conservation/pollution.

37: Swim Fabrics

Purpose
To test, sort and rank a variety of fabrics on a number of characteristics.

Resources
A collection of swimsuits of different materials including, for example, cotton, nylon and Lycra®.

The task in action
The children are asked to decide how they want to test four swimsuits to determine which is the best fabric. There is room on the copymaster for the children to draw the suits and write in the results.

Teacher help and information
Discuss with the children the important characteristics we look for in a swim fabric. For example, they may decide it needs to dry quickly, not retain water, stretch but not too much, and return to its original shape and size after stretching. They can then decide how to construct tests for these characteristics, an appropriate order for doing them, and how to determine the results.

Connections and extensions
Extend this work to studies of other materials and characteristics. For example, what materials are 'stretchy', how do we know they are and what do we use elastic materials for? What materials can support heavy 'weights'? When do we use a net and what characteristics do the materials used in nets have (include a net of oranges, fishing net, hairnet, basketball net, table tennis net, net shopping bag, mosquito net, net curtain, netting fence)?

Connect this work to investigations 32: Shoes and 72: All-weather wear.

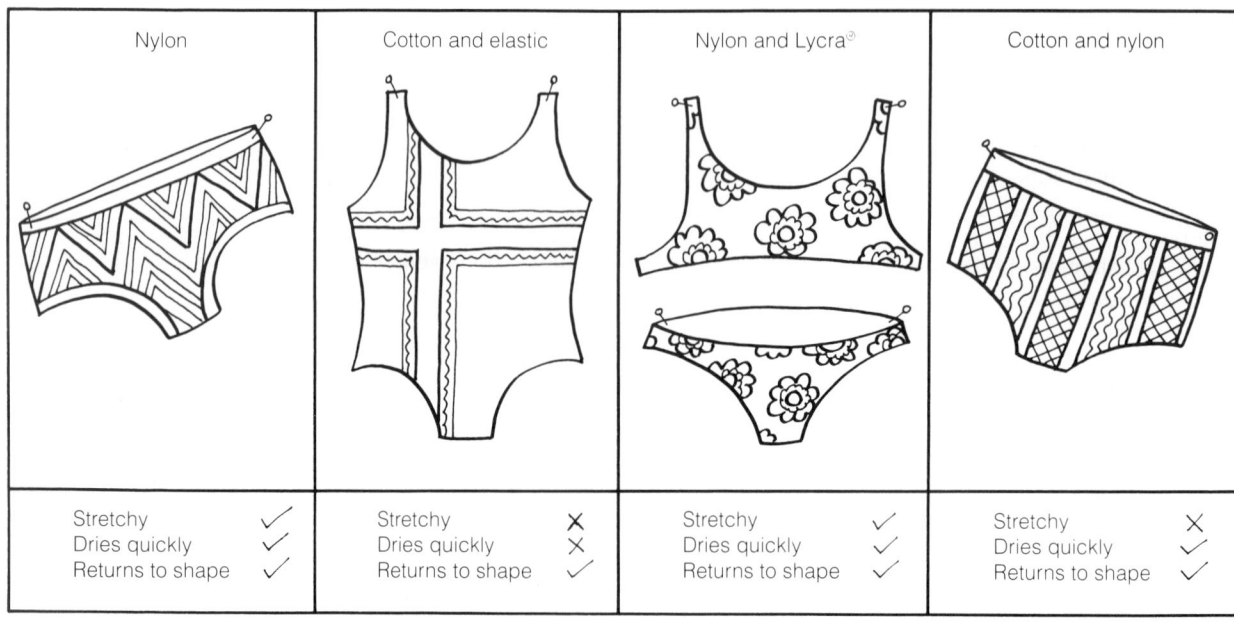

| M & P | **38: Tea Making** |

Purpose
To devise a fair test and develop some hypotheses about mixtures.

Resources
Kettle, water, teapot, tea bags, cups; milk and sugar if necessary.

The task in action
The children must devise a number of ways of making tea to test the idea that the water it is made with is fresh, boiling and not boiling too much. They are then asked to try out the tea on a panel of testers, and state their conclusions.

Teacher help and information
Be sure to observe safety measures to ensure the children do not risk being scalded. Remind them that boiling water scalds badly, but it does not need to reach boiling point before it can cause severe burns.

Connections and extensions
In this investigation children are determining whether a particular mixture meets certain criteria within a small range of conditions. Their work can be extended to look at other mixtures and compounds. For example, do cakes always rise if the proportions of fat to flour are in the same ratio? Does this hold for pastry? How much washing powder should be used for best results? On what does this amount depend?

Link this work to whole school investigation 88: Cooking.

| M & P | **39: Temperatures around School** |

Purpose
To study environmental change through temperature by allowing children to take thermometer readings and to tabulate and interpret results, discussing their practical implications.

Resources
Four thermometers; signs warning other children of the experiment to ensure the thermometers remain undisturbed.

The task in action
As instructed on the copymaster, the children can decide where to set their thermometers and when to take readings.

Teacher help and information
Show the children how to place the thermometers safely, and how to add notices to other children saying that care must be taken not to touch or tamper with the thermometers, if these are necessary. Remind the children that the thermometer readings must be taken at eye level.

Connections and extensions
Allow the children to act on suggestions they make themselves about their results. Also help the children extend the investigation by asking them to do some of the following:

- take readings and rank all parts of the school from hottest to coolest
- make a heat map of the school, using a colour code
- report on how heat could be better conserved in school.

See also other investigations about environmental changes including 54: Noises and sound proofing.

| M & P | **40: Using Light-sensitive Paper** |

Purpose
To see what happens to light-sensitive paper when placed in sunlight and to make shadow pictures.

Resources
A changing bag; light-sensitive paper; collection of objects; sheet plastic.

The task in action
As instructed on the copymaster, the children can expose a sheet of light-sensitive paper to bright sun for five minutes. They can then experiment with different objects or different timings, and discuss the effects.

Teacher help and information
The paper does need to be kept in a light-proof box and removed from the box using a changing bag or in a blacked-out room (the stock cupboard may be suitable). If the children choose fairly flat objects to lay on the paper they can anchor them with a piece of sheet plastic. This is a useful introduction to some of the technical ideas in photography. Tell the children that there are chemicals on the paper which undergo change when in light and we can prevent further change by 'fixing' the paper.

If you are unfamiliar with photographic developing seek the advice of an assistant in a camera shop. Most kits have full instructions and appropriate chemicals. Remember the health and safety rules to observe in schools. See also 'Ilford: Classroom Photography' obtainable from Ilford Ltd., 14–22 Tottenham St., London W1P 0AH.

Connections and extensions
Link this work to investigation 30: Photography.

41: Reflective Surfaces

Purpose
To find and draw some reflective surfaces as an introduction to the phenomena associated with the reflection of light.

Resources
A collection of objects made of reflective material, for example, a kettle, saucepans, spoons, metal foil and mirrors.

The task in action
The children have to draw some things they can see themselves reflected in, and the reflections produced.

Teacher help and information
Though you can provide some resources it is worth exploring what surfaces around the school offer possibilities for investigating reflections. Some reflections will be distorted. See if the children can determine whether the distortion depends on the curvature of the reflective surface.

Connections and extensions
Make sure the children know what 'reflect' means. Let them determine what is necessary for us to see a reflection. For example, can we see reflections in the dark? Can we see anything in the dark? What happens to the reflection when the light level is low? Does polishing a reflective surface change the reflection? If so, how? Do all shiny things give a reflection?

Connect this work to weekend science investigation 94: Periscope.

42: Shadow Playing

Purpose
To find out how a shadow is formed and look at the effects of moving the light source and the object casting the shadow.

Resources
Strips of wood or dowel; sheeting, string, covered table; paper and card; scissors, sticky tape and glue; bean sticks; torch or lamp; facilities for reducing light levels or blacking out the classroom.

The task in action
Using the diagram on the copymaster, the children are asked to set up a shadow play screen and put on a show. They can then try moving the torch and the puppets to see what happens to the shadows.

Teacher help and information
One screen can be made to be used by all the children, but they do all need to try individually 'playing' with the shadows the puppets make.

Connections and extensions
The weekend science investigation 91: Shadows offers you the opportunity to give the children an introduction to this topic, before they do this investigation. Links can be made to investigation 11: Seeing through.

43: Balloon Rocket

Purpose
To demonstrate that objects can be made to move by air that is under pressure.

Resources
Long balloon, balloon pump, fishing line, plastic drinking straw, sticky tape, clothes peg; seconds timer.

The task in action
The copymaster has a diagram and instructions on how to set up the experiment. The children are asked to attach a blown-up balloon to a plastic straw and then using the force of the air released from the balloon propel the balloon at speed, and up hill, along a fishing line 'cable'.

Teacher help and information
This is an impressive experiment that the children should remember easily. While it does require several pairs of hands, the children should be able to do it with minimal supervision.

Connections and extensions
Extend the work by asking the children to investigate the use we make of air pressure or the force of air in everyday life. Examples include the working of an aneroid barometer, sailing and wind surfing, and a hover craft.

44: Colour Filters

Purpose
To study the effects of colour filters on what we see.

Resources
Sticky paper or sticky paper shapes; coloured cellophanes (sweet wrappers will do).

The task in action
The children are given full instructions on the copymaster. They need to make a sticky paper picture that they view through cellophane in a variety of colours and then record the results.

Teacher help and information
This investigation gives practice in filling the cells in a table. The children can colour the cells, rather than writing the colour words if you wish.

Connections and extensions
Link this work to investigations 15: Mixing colours of light, 83: Spectrum and weekend science investigation 93: Kaleidoscope.

45: Cotton Reel Toy

Purpose
To find out about the forces at work in a cotton reel toy.

Resources
Cotton reels, elastic bands, dead matches, candle.

The task in action
Having made a toy to match the one on the copymaster the children have to experiment with it to determine what affects its movement.

Teacher help and information
The energy stored in the elastic band converts to kinetic (movement) energy and thus the band force propels the toy along. The match does need to extend beyond the edge of the cotton reel, so that the toy rocks onto the match end at each revolution.

Connections and extensions
The children could find some commercially-produced toys, like model aeroplanes, that use rubber band force and devise some experiments to do with these.
   This work links to investigation 56: Paddle boat.

46: Friction

Purpose
To explore ideas about friction in a practical context.

Resources
A collection of shoes with a variety of different kinds of sole; a grassy patch of ground; water; a piece of ice frozen in an ice tray (without compartments).

The task in action
Following the instructions on the copymaster, the children are required to set up an experiment to test the 'ground-holding' ability of a variety of kinds of shoe soles, devise a scale for results and present their findings.

Teacher help and information
Help the children to work out a systematic strategy. Discuss the fact that what they do may be a useful exploratory experiment, but not a 'fair test'. Talk about what a shoe manufacturer might do to create such a test. If the work is to be displayed, the results could form a row of footprints, or paper cut into shoe sole shapes could be used to display results.

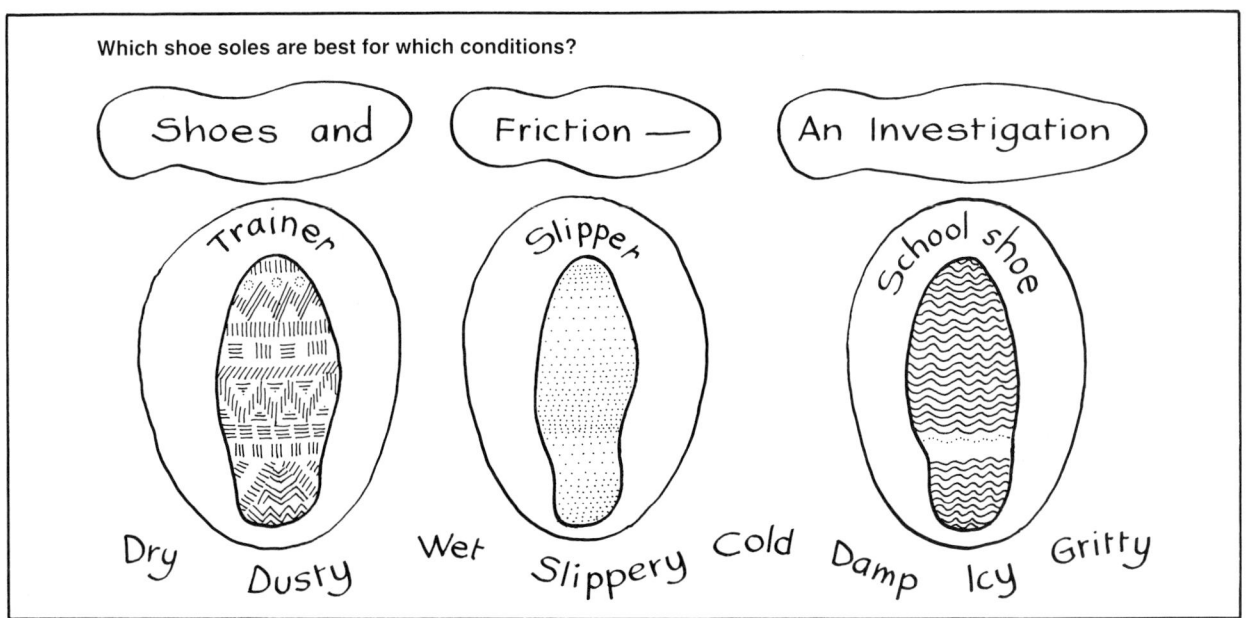

Connections and extensions
Extend the children's work by getting information about a number of makes of car tyre, and comparing the road-holding claims of their manufacturers. Ask the children to explore all the sports, games and toys where friction or lack of it plays a part, for example, curling, roller skating and the playground slide.

Link this work to investigations 32: Shoes and 47: Friction car and trailer.

47: Friction Car and Trailer

Purpose
To explore the force needed to move a given load.

Resources
A friction car; a trailer which fixes (or can be tied) to the car; cargo.

The task in action
The children should first establish the distance the friction car will travel without any external loading. They should consider the idea of a 'fair test' in respect of how they power the car for each test. They should try a number of tests and obtain the average. The effect of the addition of a trailer should then be explored. The trailer can then be progressively loaded and trials repeated.

Teacher help and information
The intention in using a friction car is that there will be a good chance that the energy stored in the car for each test will be roughly the same. This will mean that children can 'charge' the car with energy each time and assume that the distance covered will then be affected by the mass of the trailer and/or the cargo used.

Connections and extensions
Discuss the idea of haulage involved in the capacity of lorries of different types, including technical descriptions such as given axle loadings. This could also be explored with trains and ships. Challenge the children to explore motion, inertia and momentum and begin some preliminary thinking about possible connections between distance, speed and time.

Link this work to investigation 46: Friction.

48: Good Conductors

Purpose
To find what sorts of things conduct electricity.

Resources
Circuit wire, 4.5 volt battery, lamp in a lamp holder, crocodile clips; access to a variety of things to attach to the clips.

The task in action
The children can make a circuit and try a number of objects to complete it. They can note which allow the current to pass and which do not.

Teacher help and information
If the children have adequate resources, they should be able to do this investigation with little help and discover that some metals conduct electricity readily.

Connections and extensions
Link this work to other circuit investigations including investigation 52: Model theatre.

49: Make a Stringed Instrument

Purpose
To confirm that in stringed instruments the strings and the instrument vibrate to produce sounds.

Resources
'Junk' materials; scissors, cardboard, string, rubber bands; other resources the children require for their designs.

The task in action
The children have to invent an instrument with one or more strings and test out their instruments to see if they can change the pitch of notes produced.

Teacher help and information
Collect a huge bank of resources before the children begin so that they are not frustrated in attempts to build their designs.

Connections and extensions
Link this work to investigation 53: Musical instruments.

50: Mass and Volume

Purpose
To compare the masses and volumes of a variety of objects.

Resources
A wide variety of objects appropriate for weighing on a classroom balance; balances; some pairs of objects of similar volume but different mass; large container of water (preferably transparent, like an aquarium or vivarium empty of inhabitants); sticky labels, pencils; tongs to retrieve sunken objects.

The task in action
The children have to find three pairs of things that weigh the same but have different shapes and sizes, and then three pairs having the same shape and size but different masses. They then examine any differences in water displacement by the objects as an index of volume differences.

Teacher help and information
The children may need some hints in their search for what is appropriate. Items of similar shape and size but different mass can be difficult to find; you may have building blocks of similar dimensions but made of, say, wood and plastic. A full and empty drink carton or can (with the holes taped over), and food packaging that is immersible in water may be useful. When trying to find how much water each object displaces you will need to prod with a pencil those objects that float so they go under the water. Small sticky labels on the outside of the container, if it is transparent, can help determine differences in water level.

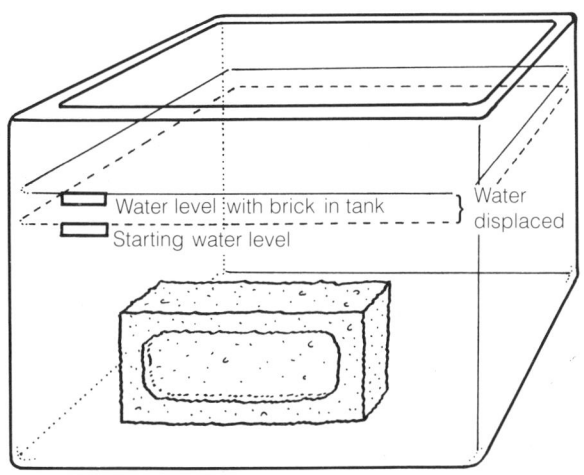

Connections and extensions
Link this work to investigation 74: Boats.

51: Möbius Band

Purpose
To explore the idea of surfaces through using a Möbius band.

Resources
Squared paper (5 mm), wax crayons, sticky tape.

The task in action
The copymaster offers detailed steps in the construction and exploration of the Möbius band.

Teacher help and information
The Möbius band offers an intriguing investigation because the effects obtained are curious. The idea of having a continuous band of material which appears to have only one surface is challenging. The Möbius band is used in industrial and agricultural applications as a means of evening out the wear on bands and belts. When you next see machinery which employs belts to transmit movement you may see that these belts have a twist in them – they are Möbius bands.

Connections and extensions
Take the children to industrial museums, heritage centres or old agricultural machinery displays. They can see many applications of science and technology including the Möbius band.

52: Model Theatre

Purpose
To create an electrical circuit and use it in a practical setting.

Resources
Circuit wire, 4.5 volt battery, lamp and lamp holder; shoe box, card, scissors, drawing materials.

The task in action
The copymaster presents the problem: namely to make a spotlight to light part of the stage in a shoe box production. Children have to compile instructions to show how they made their theatres.

Teacher help and information
Give the children time to see this through. The finished theatres would make an appealing display for a parents' evening or in the entrance hall.

Connections and extensions
Link this work to other circuitry investigations, including investigations 48: Good conductors and 76: Electricity and magnetism.

53: Musical Instruments

Purpose
To study the methods by which sounds are produced on a variety of musical instruments and to learn that to have sound there must be vibration.

Resources
A variety of musical instruments and some people who can play them.

The task in action
By watching, listening to and examining instruments, and listening to musicians describing and showing how they are played, the children can work out how the sounds are produced and write in the required information below the appropriate pictures on the copymaster.

Teacher help and information
Help the children distinguish between woodwind, brass, percussion and stringed instruments. Woodwind and brass are all wind, that is use only the breath. Brass instruments are usually made solely from brass although some instruments have different finishes. Some wind instruments have a reed which vibrates when blown over and sets the air column in the instrument vibrating. Percussion instruments are struck to set the vibration going and stringed instruments are plucked or scraped. All instruments, even electronic ones, have to create vibration of the air, in order to transmit sound.

Connections and extensions
Try making some musical instruments using card, string, wooden boxes, bottles, tubes of metal, plastic bottles and so on. Help the children to find out about musical scales, tempo and amplitude.

Link this work to investigation 49: Make a stringed instrument.

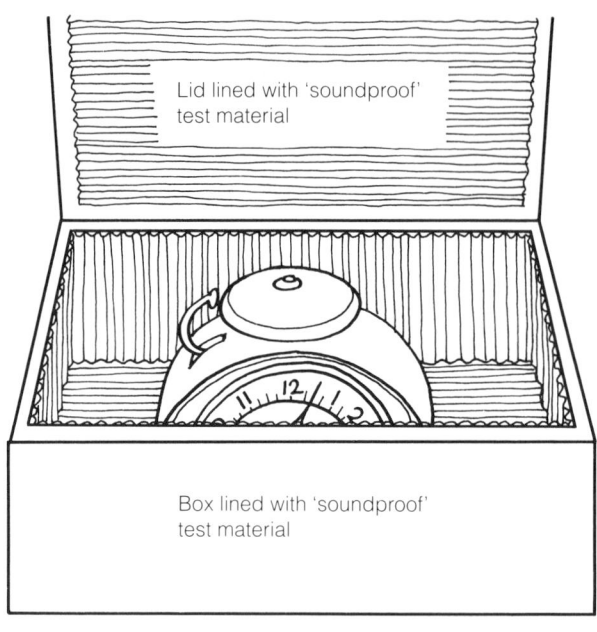

If sound can be heard through the closed box how far away can it still be heard?

54: Noises and Sound proofing

Purpose
To investigate which materials sound does not pass through easily.

Resources
These will depend on the kinds of materials the children decide they want to test, but could include, for example, polystyrene ceiling tiles, bricks, wood, fabrics, plastic sheet and corrugated card.

The task in action
The children need to collect information about the kinds of noise heard around the school and its location. They can then test which of a variety of materials do not let sound through and use this information to devise a plan about noise reduction.

Teacher help and information
The children may need to complete several copies of the data collection sheet at different times of the day, to get a 'feel' for the school's noisy locations. You may have to advise on the conditions for experimentation because the children will need to isolate the noise they use for the tests and then decide how to set up the soundproof materials. Here is one suggestion that could be tried.

Connections and extensions
Link this to other work on environmental change, for example, investigation 39: Temperatures around school. One of the extensions to that investigation is to make a 'heat map' of the school. Armed with a tape recorder which indicates sound levels, the children could try creating a 'sound map' of the school.

55: Optical Illusions

Purpose
To explore a range of situations where we can be deceived by optical illusions and to seek explanations for these.

Resources
Books about optical illusions.

The task in action
The children are asked to try some optical illusions, find out how they work, and find some more.

Teacher help and information
The reasons we are 'fooled' vary from one illusion to another. In some, like the lines on the copymaster, it is the juxtaposition of lines and shapes that defeat our brains. In others the attempt by both eyes to make the one image (which is what our stereoscopic vision gives us) can make parts of a picture fuse. Yet others rely on the fact that an image on the retina lasts a fraction of a second after the stimulus has moved (animated film depends on this image retention).

Connections and extensions
The children can extend this work by looking at conjuring tricks to see if any of these rely on fooling the eye and therefore the brain, and at old toys like the zeotrope and thaumatrope that both use optical effects. Flicker and roller books also depend on image retention to work.

Link this work to investigation 30: Photography and weekend science investigation 94: Periscope (though this is not illusory, the ability to 'bend' light so that you can see round corners is certainly surprising).

56: Paddle Boat

Purpose
To find out about the forces at work in a paddle boat.

Resources
Balsa wood; tools to cut the wood; tacks, elastic bands; tank or sink of water.

The task in action
There is a picture of a prototype paddle boat on the copymaster. There are also some key questions to help the children focus their thinking and determine whether the turns of the band, the direction of the turns and the size of the paddle can affect the motion of the boat.

Teacher help and information
Give the children time to play with their inventions before they determine the answers to the questions on the copymaster.

Connections and extensions
Extend this work by observing the phenomenon of momentum (momentum is mass × velocity). Let the children note that the boat keeps going after the band has unwound. Does a larger boat or a boat with more turns to the band keep going for longer?
Link this work to investigation 45: Cotton Reel Toy.

57: Paper Aeroplanes

Purpose
To think about the forces exerted on a paper aeroplane and to modify the force to increase the distance travelled.

Resources
A4 paper; measuring tape and chalk; scissors, paper clips, Plasticine®.

The task in action
The children are required to follow the instructions for making a paper aeroplane that are on the copymaster, and produce a full report on their experiments.

Teacher help and information
Offer the children advice about the systematic recording of distances travelled and of modifications made. Suggest that they may like to make up a new aeroplane for every trial, and label and write notes on each.

Connections and extensions
Extend the work by helping the children arrange a comparative display, showing all their modifications.
Link this work to investigation 31: Seed dispersal 2.

58: Poles of a Magnet

Purpose
To find out the polarity of magnets in a pair of magnetic toys.

Resources
Magnetic toys, which can be found in toy shops (they often come in pairs and are in animal shapes of about 3 cm long); a clamp and string will also be helpful; a knowledge of which way is north in the classroom.

The task in action
The children are asked to determine the polarity of the magnets in the toys and say how they found this out.

Teacher help and information
If the children play with the toys they will be able to get them to attract and repel one another. This tells them

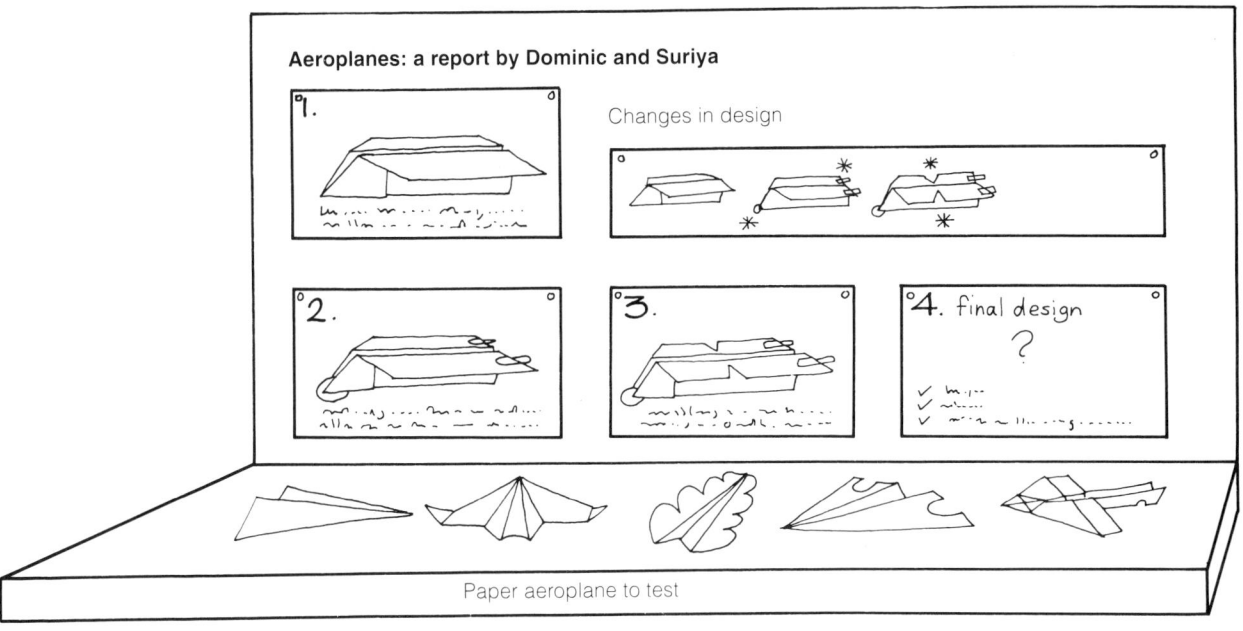
Paper aeroplane to test

which are opposite poles (attract) but not which one is north and which south. If one of the toys is suspended so that it swings freely it will come to lie in a north–south direction in the earth's magnetic field. This is just what a compass needle does. The polarity of one of the toys should enable the children to deduce that of the other.

Connections and extensions
Link this work to investigation 14: Magnetic attraction and 76: Electricity and magnetism.

 59: Puck Game

Purpose
To look at what happens to the motion of an object when force is applied from a new direction.

Resources
Jar lids like those for jam or coffee jars; marbles.

The task in action
Several marbles, trapped under a jar lid, move freely across a polished floor. The children are asked to see what happens when two of these pucks collide and use the knowledge they gain to design and play a puck game.

Teacher help and information
If a moving puck collides with a stationary one the moving puck will change direction. It does so in a regular way such that the angle at which it hits the stationary one is equal to the angle at which it moves off again. The stationary puck may also move away. Where both pucks are moving, the distances that they move after impact will depend on their speeds as well as directions. The game can make use of this phenomenon, and can be about knocking an opponent's puck, clearing the board, reaching a target or some other idea of the children's invention.

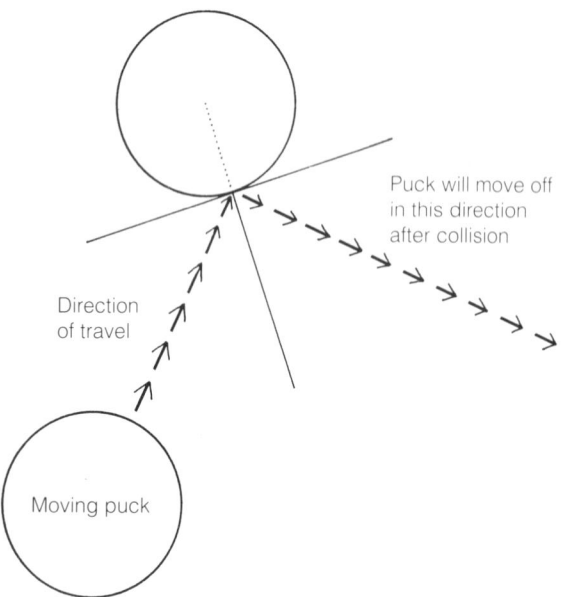

Connections and extensions
The children can explore which games use collisions like these as an important aspect of the game. Examples include snooker, billiards, curling, bowls, ice hockey and squash.

 60: Pulleys

Purpose
To find out whether pulleys make lifting easier and whether they give any mechanical advantage.

Resources
Cotton reels, string, wire coat hangers, wire cutters; pebbles and other masses to try on the pulley; support for the pulley (rail, string or clamp); newton-meter.

The task in action
The children have to make a pulley, work out the distance they must pull to raise a mass a measured distance, and then make a complex pulley and do the same experiment.

Teacher help and information
The children will need your help in cutting the hangers. Help them also to pull carefully in one direction. One way of marking the length of pull is to do the experiment close to a wall on which a piece of backing paper is stuck. Mark where the pull starts, the line of pull and the finishing point. Use a bag of sugar as a standard weight and compare the difference in sensation between lifting the bag with a simple pulley compared with a double (or more complex) pulley. Useful discussion about 'effort' should ensue. The children should find that a complex pulley offers mechanical advantage (that is it means less work to achieve more lift than a simple pulley).

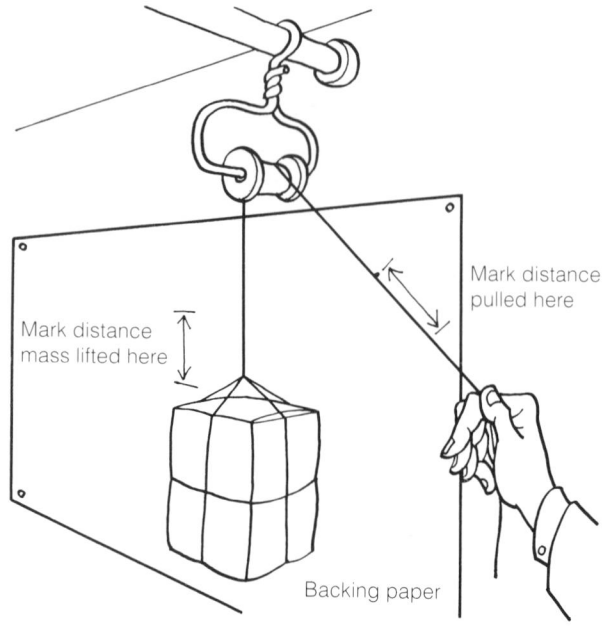

Connections and extensions
This work can be linked to a variety of activities to do with machines and technology. Invite some members of the business community to school to share information about some of the tools that they use in their work. Examples of businesses to approach are builders, lift and hoist manufacturers, car repairers and warehouse managers.

61: Sailing

Purpose
To make paper sails of different shapes and sizes and to find which works best for a model boat.

Resources
Margarine tubs, Plasticine®, lolly sticks, paper, scissors, sticky tape or glue, rulers.

The task in action
The children are invited to make a boat, cut out sails of various sizes and shapes and determine, by any means they suggest, which is the best sail.

Teacher help and information
Discuss with the children what constitutes a 'fair' test and whether theirs is fair.

Connections and extensions
The boats are moved by the force of the air blown onto them. This work could therefore be linked to other investigations on forces, for example, investigations 74: Boats, 18: Teddy moves and 84: Speed and distance.

62: Sand Clock

Purpose
To make a sand clock and use it as a timing device.

Resources
These will depend on the designs the children like to try, but offer a wide range of junk materials including cans, cartons, bags and boxes, plastic bottles, corks and stoppers, card, straws and sand; scissors and a bodkin or something similar that will make a small hole.

The task in action
The copymaster is intended as a record of production modifications to show how the sand clock works.

Teacher help and information
The most important work in this investigation is the 'trial and improvement' stage to get the invention to work.

Connections and extensions
Link to other time-keeping devices like that in investigation 68: Water clock.

63: See-saw

Purpose
To 'play' with the forces at work in a see-saw and to begin to understand that it is a range of forces that affect the position and movement of objects, and to learn something about the operation of levers.

Resources
A piece of wood suitable for sitting toys on: a prism-shaped box or building block to use as the fulcrum or make one using corrugated card, parcel tape and scissors; toys; cut-down plastic bottles as seats; PVA glue.

The task in action
The child must make a see-saw, find some toys to go on the see-saw, draw them and then get the see-saw to balance.

Teacher help and information
The children may need help with the construction of the see-saw. It works quite well when three pieces of corrugated card are stapled together. The fulcrum can be made from rectangles of card taped together to make a triangular prism. The bottoms cut from plastic squash or water bottles make good seats. Use the children's trials as opportunities to introduce concepts such as the force of gravity (which pulls the see-saw and toys to the ground), the 'weight' (or more correctly mass) of the toys and the idea that the see-saw can have a fulcrum that is *not* at the centre. Talk about what happens when the children themselves are on a see-saw.

Connections and extensions
This work links to ideas about levers. You might be able to extend the discussion into the identification of a range of common tools that use levers. These include scissors, wheel barrows, gardening shears, arms (bending at the elbow) and hinges.

64: Signalling – Morse

Purpose
To learn how an electrical circuit can be used to send messages and to investigate Morse code.

Resources
Circuit wire, 4.5 volt batteries, lamps in lamp holders or buzzers, simple switches that can be home-made.

The task in action
The children need to create a lamp or buzzer circuit, use it to convey a message and then find out all they can about Morse, so that they can send a message using this code.

Teacher help and information
Morse is the code invented for use on the electric telegraph. It comprises long (dash) and short (dot) signals, each letter of the alphabet and each numeral having a different configuration: SOS is three dots, three dashes, three dots.

Connections and extensions
Link this investigation to investigation 81: Signalling – Lighthouses.

65: Stopping Force

Purpose
To show that the greater the mass of a moving object, the more force is needed to stop it.

Resources
Long bench or plank and something to prop it up with so that it will make a ramp; toy cars each of a different mass; a balloon pump; a block of balsa wood; strong sticky tape.

The task in action
On the copymaster is a diagram of the apparatus. The children have to record how far a range of toy cars placed on a ramp push a balsa wood block.

Teacher help and information
The children's results should reveal that heavier cars push the block further. Remind the children to place each car at the top of the ramp (in the same position) so that it moves under gravitational force and not to push start the car. This will offer the same conditions for each vehicle. If it is difficult to rank the cars in terms of mass, help the children to weigh them.

Connections and extensions
If it is possible using the resources in the classroom the children could try to find out whether wheel size has any effect on the stopping force of a toy car when the mass is constant.

66: Sundials

Purpose
To make and test out a sundial and thereby understand the use we can make of the sun's elevation in the sky to tell the time.

Resources
Access to pictures of sundials, or actual sundials in gardens or a garden centre; reference material showing how a sundial works; latitude location of the school; cardboard, protractors, scissors; compass; sunshine.

The task in action
The children are required to carry through the investigation from the stage of finding out how a sundial works to designing and constructing one that works.

Teacher help and information
The pointer on a sundial needs to be a right-angled triangle with an angle of inclination the same as the latitude of your location. The dial is calibrated by setting the pointer at north each time the sundial is taken outside.

Connections and extensions
Link this work to other ways of keeping time that are pre-mechanised, for example, investigations 62: Sand clock and 68: Water clock.

67: Using Air Pressure

Purpose
To show that we can use air pressure to create sensitive scientific instruments.

Resources
Balloon pump, balloon, cardboard box, clip or clothes peg, elastic band, clamp; transparent plastic tubing and funnel to fit the end of the tubing; jug of water.

The task in action
Using the instructions on the copymaster, the children are invited to build a piece of apparatus that uses air pressure to detect differences in mass.

Teacher help and information
Clamping the neck of the balloon and fixing it to the tubing may be aspects of the setting up that need your help. You may also like to add a little food colour to the water so that it is easier to see in the tube.

Connections and extensions
Air pressure is used in a variety of machines. The children can collect together the names of as many machines as they can. The pressure of air is measured by the aneroid barometer. The children can find out how this works.

68: Water Clock

Purpose
To make a timer to measure seconds or minutes using water.

Resources
As in investigation 62: Sand clock, give the children access to a wide variety of junk modelling materials. Include plenty of plastics as these are impermeable to water.

The task in action
The copymaster is a record sheet for modifications necessary to produce a working timer.

Teacher help and information
The children may need your help in experimenting with hole sizes to permit the flow of water to match the time scale.

Connections and extensions
Link this work to other time-keeping investigations including investigation 62: Sand clock.

69: Weighing Paper

Purpose
To let children have the opportunity to choose and use appropriate measuring equipment and units to solve a problem, in this case the weight of a single sheet of paper.

Resources
Books; loose A4 paper; a variety of balances; non-standard things used in weighing and a range of standard masses; calculators.

The task in action
The children could work in twos to choose and try out their chosen equipment to weigh paper, and from their results determine the 'weight' of one sheet.

Teacher help and information
Help the children to plan a strategy, assess what is available, make a systematic record of what they do and clearly state their findings. They can use any kind of appropriate balance and any single kind of thing to weigh with; determining the solution by using, for example, small fractions of a conker (perhaps to two or three decimal places).

Connections and extensions
Let the children devise further challenges involving choosing equipment appropriate for a challenge. For example, can they determine the following:

- the mass of all the leaves on one of the playground trees?
- the mass of all the brown-eyed girls in school?
- how much water in a puddle?
- how many jars of coffee powder the teachers will use in a term?
- the number of fleeces necessary to make all the dinner ladies a jumper each?

70: Wheels

Purpose
To find out some of the decisions that can be made about the number, size and placing of wheels on a vehicle, and how these decisions affect the vehicle's motion.

Resources
Junk materials suitable for making wheeled trucks, for example, a variety of packaging; card, glue, parcel tape, scissors.

The task in action
The copymaster is intended to stimulate the children's own decisions about the enquiries they make about wheels.

Teacher help and information
To make wheels that move freely on a junk model is a design problem. If the children have difficulty discuss 'housing' the axle in special carriers which could be made from a drinking straw, as here:

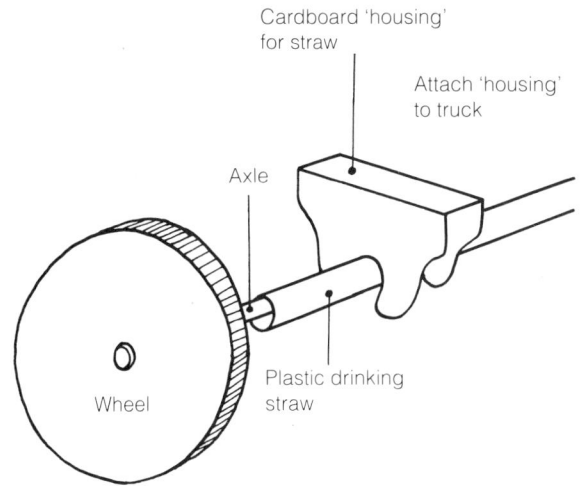

To glean communicable results the children will need to record their findings systematically.

Connections and extensions
The motion of a wheel can be shown to be like that of a wave. Get the children to stick a label on a wheel edge and mark on a paper strip the positions of the label as the wheel goes around.

Link this work to investigation 84: Speed and distance, where wheel size may be a factor to consider.

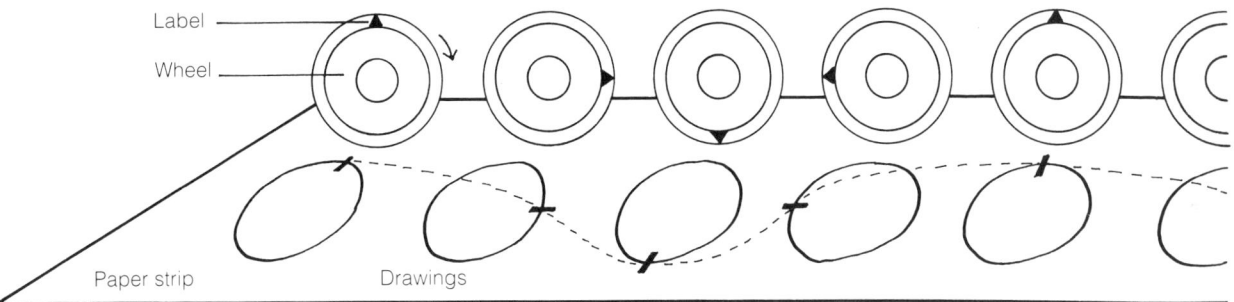

Section C: Level 5

71: Fingerprints
LP & LT

Purpose
To discuss the idea of individual differences and the uniqueness of fingerprints.

Resources
Ink pads; rough paper; washing facilities.

The task in action
The children have full instructions for making and comparing fingerprints on the copymaster. Their results should provide the evidence to prove the uniqueness of fingerprints.

Teacher help and information
This investigation needs to be carefully done to get clear prints and can be messy if unsupervised.

Connections and extensions
If there are identical twins in school, see if the children can take their prints and inspect them.
Connect to other investigations about similarities and differences.

72: All-weather Wear
M & P

Purpose
To test out the idea that we choose materials for a purpose and to identify some of the characteristics used in making a choice.

Resources
Catalogues and advertisements for clothes worn for outdoor sports including hill-walking, mountaineering and sailing, and for fastenings used on these kinds of clothes; a wide variety of fabric samples; access to water and other resources determined by the experiments the children decide to set up.

The task in action
The children have to design a jacket suitable for all-weather outdoor wear, having tested fabrics and examined and discussed fastenings. The copymaster is a record of decisions that affected the final decision.

Teacher help and information
The children may need your help in setting up tests that are practical in a classroom setting.

Connections and extensions
Link this work to investigations 32: Shoes and 37: Swim fabrics. Extend what the children have done by getting them to research the qualities looked for in other materials used in special conditions, for example, space travel or deep sea diving, and for special jobs like hard hats for wear on building sites, visors worn in situations where the eyes are at risk, and protective sportswear like knee pads.

73: Raindrops
M & P   PP

Purpose
To investigate drops of rain and estimate how much water is in a drop, what its spread is, and extrapolate from these figures to some large-scale estimates. There is also the opportunity to generate new hypotheses and try to test them.

Resources
Rain; sugar paper, water, eye dropper, medicine cup or spoon; millimetre ruler; washing-up bowl, washing-up liquid, soap, tea-bag; calculators may help in working out the rainfall.

The task in action
Detailed instructions are given to the children on the copymaster. They need to look at the spread of a raindrop and try to estimate how much water may be in one drop. They then try to determine how much rain falls on the playground in one minute. Finally they have to invent some more experiments to do with raindrops.

Teacher help and information
This is a truly open-ended investigation. There are no 'right answers' in this work but there are 'right procedures'. The ideas behind a fair test and being a scientist are central to the work. So give the children time to develop new hypotheses and carry them forward in experimentation as long as this is fruitful.

Connections and extensions
The children may wish to extend this work by looking at, for example, solubility, water purity, water sources, the water cycle and water pressure.
Link this work to investigations 35: Drink in the desert and 36: Filtering water.

74: Boats
M & P   PP

Purpose
To explore the effect of shape on floating and sinking.

Resources
Plasticine®; kitchen foil; bowl or tank of water.

The task in action
Ask the children to make spheres of the Plasticine® and the kitchen foil and get them to drop the spheres into the water to see what happens. Suggest they try compressing the kitchen foil as hard as possible – does this affect the results? Having used the Plasticine® and foil in this way now get the children to change the shape of the Plasticine® and foil in order to see whether they can make them float.

Teacher help and information
Floating is dependent on the floating object having a density less than the density of water. A 'boat' shape (foil and air) will be less dense than water. It will float, displacing its own 'weight' of water.

Connections and extensions
Link this to investigation 61: Sailing.
Extend this work by finding out about shipbuilding, the Plimsoll line and primitive boats like coracles and canoes.

The task in action
Make a range of springs by winding different thicknesses of wire around pencils. Suspend each spring in turn and mark its starting length and stretch length, when different masses are suspended from it. Test the springs for the 'mass' that they will support before they are distorted.

Teacher help and information
The 'weights' should be standard in the sense that they are equivalent but they do not need to be standard weights, in other words you could use, for example, plastic blocks. A *distorted* spring is one that fails to return to its original length after stretching.

Connections and extensions
Using cylinders thicker than pencils you can explore the effects, if any, of 'fatter' springs. The children could try plotting a graph of 'weight' against the stretched length of spring. They will see that the slope of the graph changes markedly when the spring is stretched beyond its elastic limits.

75: Elasticity of Springs

Purpose
To explore the stretch and rebound of a variety of springs.

Resources
A range of wires of different thicknesses (but all must be readily bendable); pencils of the same width; small 'weights'; clamps or cup hooks from which to suspend the springs; backing paper.

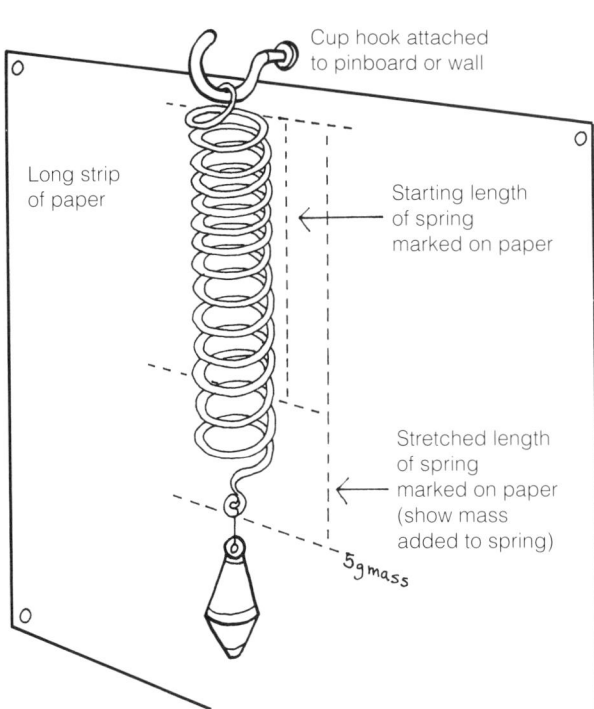

76: Electricity and Magnetism

Purpose
To show the magnetic effects of an electric current.

Resources
Copper wire, large nails, two 4.5 volt batteries connected in series, switch; paper clips and other small objects that can be attracted by a magnet.

The task in action
Full instructions appear on the copymaster, though it is assumed the child can connect a circuit correctly. It should be possible to magnetise a nail by passing an electric current through wire wound around the nail. Some further experiments are suggested on the copymaster.

Teacher help and information
The copymaster shows the wire wound around the nail several times. In reality the wire may need to be wound round *more* times than that shown. Check that the children can connect the batteries in series.

Connections and extensions
Let the children generate new hypotheses that they can test, once they have completed those on the copymaster. Ask the children to investigate the commercial uses of this phenomenon, which include crane pick-ups in used car dumps.
Link this work to investigation 82: Skip.

77: Hydraulics

Purpose
To explore the ideas associated with hydraulic pressure.

Resources
Plastic bottles like those that hold washing-up liquid; plastic tubing to fit the nozzles of the bottles; transparent plastic bottle with bottom removed; stopper with a central hole to take the tubing; cork mat.

The task in action
With a washing-up liquid bottle filled with water for each trial, the children should see what the effects are of a gentle squeeze, a firm squeeze and a hard squeeze. This should be done outdoors and under supervision. Having discussed their findings the children should then connect a bottle (which again needs refilling for each trial) to a plastic tube. This tube is inserted into a plastic bottle with the bottom removed as shown on the copymaster. The cut plastic bottle should then be half filled with water – it will need supporting. The children can try a range of firmness of squeeze on the washing-up liquid bottle and observe the movement of a cork mat put to float on the surface of the water in the plastic bottle. Does the firmness of squeeze affect the movement of the cork mat?

Teacher help and information
The use of hydraulics depends upon the fact that a liquid cannot be compressed. Applying pressure to a liquid in a container causes the pressure to be exerted on the walls of the container. If there are no outlets and the pressure is maintained then it is likely that the container will burst.

The principle of hydraulics is used in a range of machines. Of these, the car is probably the most common. Brake fluid fills pipes connected to the brakes and depression of the brake pedal causes pressure to be applied to the fluid which transmits that pressure to pistons which in turn move the brake pads or discs.

Connections and extensions
The children can look for applications of hydraulics in machines. The idea of pressure can be explored with gases too and this could lead to an investigation of pneumatics. Lego Technic® offers kits which make use of pneumatics. This work can be linked to work on water pressure.

78: Lock Gates

Purpose
To study the work of lock gates as examples of energy transfer and levers, and to find out some of the properties of liquids, using water as an example.

Resources
Real lock gates and canal safety information.

The task in action
Following the suggestions on the copymaster the children should work out possible reasons for the features of lock gates.

Teacher help and information
See if the children can generate a number of hypotheses about the features of lock gates, involving their observations concerning, for example, the following:

- hinges can be made to operate through a right angle
- water exerts pressure
- liquids 'seek their own level'
- teeth set at an angle avoid slippage
- human energy in turning the winch is transferred to a system of cogs working in different directions enabling the sluices to lift.

Connections and extensions
Let the children revise what they have learned by making models to replicate winches and sluices from construction toys. Ask the children to find out how the turn of a car steering wheel enables the car to change direction.

79: Pelican Crossing

Purpose
To study the siting and pattern of lights and sounds at a pelican crossing and suggest possible improvements to these crossings.

Resources
A pelican crossing; plenty of adult supervision; a copy of the highway code.

The task in action
The children must study and then replicate the pattern of lights and sounds for pedestrians and drivers at a pelican crossing. They are then invited to suggest modifications, particularly with partially-sighted or disabled people in mind.

Teacher help and information
You may consider it a good idea to tell the local police of the timing of your investigation, in case they would like to send a constable to help at the crossing. Help the children to be ambitious in their suggestions. For example, they could introduce additional sounds, give pedestrians sight of what the traffic lights are also indicating, have sensor driven 'pelican travellers' in which handicapped people can sit to cross the road, and so on.

Connections and extensions
See if the children can build model circuits to show what happens at their crossing. Try setting out logic gate diagrams to explain the course of events. Ask the children to design an automatic barrier that can be set up on a model railway circuit, enabling model people or cars to cross the track safely.

80: Pendulum

Purpose
To experiment with a pendulum and find out some of the factors that affect its swing.

Resources
String, clamp or wall mounted cup hook, backing paper sheet; one-minute timer; buttons, washers and other things that could be easily tied to the string; protractor.

The task in action
The children are required to carry through some experiments to test a series of hypotheses that they have written down about pendulums. Conclusions can be recorded on the copymaster.

Teacher help and information
A backing paper hung up behind the pendulum will enable the children to mark the starting point of the arc and the length of the string.

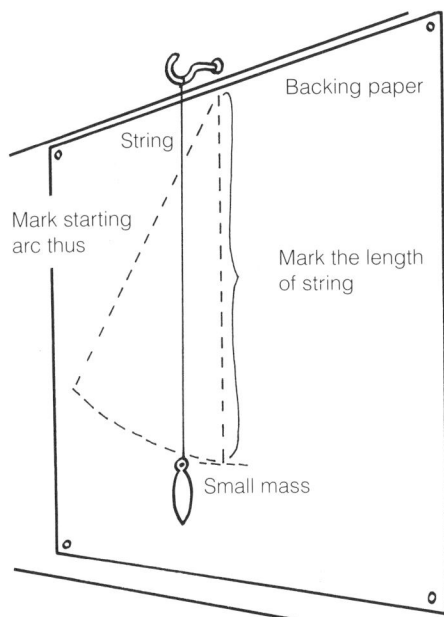

Connections and extensions
Extend by exploring how a metronome works and then use the same principles to create a pendulum timer.

81: Signalling – Lighthouses

Purpose
To look at the use of light as a signal, determine how lighthouse flashes are produced and find the pattern of flashes for a specific lighthouse.

Resources
Battery-operated lantern torch; cylinder of card; navigation maps of the nearest coast to the school, showing lighthouses and their patterns of flashing (books for sailors on navigation may be helpful).

The task in action
The child has to look up and decipher the pattern of light flashes for a particular lighthouse and then try to demonstrate how the light is 'flashed', using the pictures on the copymaster to help.

Teacher help and information
To a sailor a lighthouse 'flash' is the time when a period of darkness between each beam of light is longer than the period of light. Where the period of light is greater the light is said to be 'occulting'. Charts give information for each lighthouse. For example, Casquets lighthouse off Alderney has this label: Gp.Fl. (5) 30 sec. 120ft. 17m. This means there is a group of 5 flashes every 30 seconds, the light is 120 feet high and can be seen from 17 miles.

Connections and extensions
Link this work to investigation 64: Signalling – Morse.

82: Skip

Purpose
To demonstrate the link between magnetism and electricity using the earth's magnetic field.

Resources
Long piece of insulated circuit wire and a sensitive galvanometer.

The task in action
As instructed on the copymaster, the child has to skip with the wire, while both ends are connected to a galvanometer, and then report on what happens.

Teacher help and information
The children should find that the pointer on the galvanometer indicates that a small electric current is flowing in the wire. A galvanometer detects electric currents by their magnetic effects. When the wire is swung through the earth's magnetic field a small current is created in the wire.

Connections and extensions
Connect this work to investigation 76: Electricity and magnetism.

83: Spectrum

Purpose
To explore the spectrum of visible light.

Resources
Water, beakers, washing-up liquid, small hoops of wire; torch, card, scissors, sticky paper; darkened room; glass prisms.

The task in action
The children should play at bubble making and then create a narrow light beam that they can shine through one and then two prisms.

Teacher help and information
Detergent bubbles should show rainbow colours. White light, shone through a prism, can be refracted so that it breaks into its constituent colours (each has a slightly different wavelength and is refracted differently). The colours are those in the rainbow: violet, indigo, blue, green, yellow, orange, red. White light can be 'reconstituted' by passing the rainbow colours through another prism. Rainbows occur when thousands of raindrops act like prisms when the sun shines through them.

Connections and extensions
Children can compare the effects of refraction with those of reflection of light as in investigation 15: Mixing colours of light.

84: Speed and Distance

Purpose
To explore the connection between distance and speed.

Resources
A ramp; toy cars; tape measure; chalk.

The task in action
The children need to set up a ramp at a fixed angle and with sufficient floor space for the moving toy car to come to a rest without hitting anything. They should take a number of measures of distance travelled by the car from half way up the ramp and the top of the ramp. These can then be averaged.

Teacher help and information
Different groups of children can compare their results. If different cars are used the results may be used to identify variables such as the masses of the cars, their lengths and the sizes of their wheels.

Connections and extensions
See investigation 70: Wheels.
The ideas generated could be used in the whole school investigation 89: Play safe, when discussing road safety.

Whole school investigations

Planning work across the whole school or department makes it possible to tackle investigations that take in work at a range of Levels. The work can be undertaken by, for example, a number of children from a variety of age groups, a number of whole classes or the whole school. The results of work done in this way can be offered in a variety of ways including:

- a whole school display, taking in space in every classroom
- a visitor display in the public areas of the school like the entrance hall
- an exemplar display for the staff room.

There follow some examples of the kinds of topics that lend themselves to a 'whole school' approach, and some of the ways of managing the outcomes. Copymasters are included on which some of the children can do their recording.

85: Science in a Rhyme

Purpose
To use a children's rhyme as a starting point to make scientific investigations about its contents.

Resources
Books of nursery rhymes and other traditional rhymes and songs.

The task in action
Ask each group or each class to choose one or more rhymes to investigate. Ask some older children to collate suggestions so that all classes do not choose the same rhymes. Have planning meetings to determine starting experiments. Carry them through and follow up the lines of enquiry. The copymaster is a sheet with a decorative border that the children can write on.

Teacher help and information
Try to help the children to be as expansive as possible in their plans. For example, 'Little Miss Muffet' might yield the following suggestions:

- what are curds and whey?
- how can we make it?
- what does it smell/taste like?
- why would Miss Muffet be asked to eat it?
- what is a tuffet?
- can we make a stable tuffet?
- what kinds of spiders are there?
- what proportion of children in the school are afraid of spiders?
- are more or fewer boys than girls frightened of spiders?
- does fear of spiders have any substance?
- do spiders like curds and whey?
- do spiders like girls?

And to show that this is not the only rhyme to spark a list of enquiries, the list for 'Jack and Jill' might run like this:

- can you get water at the top of a hill?
- what kinds of ways are there for raising water from the ground?
- is there water everywhere under the ground?
- what materials might a pail be made from?
- what is a good shape for ease of carrying?
- was Jack's recipe for mending his head a good one?
- if so, how does the remedy work?

Connections and extensions
The rhymes worked on are the common theme, though you may choose a theme within them like 'food and drink' (plum pies, piemen, fat and lean, blackbird pie, royal butter) or 'movement in rhyme'.

The children's work can be extended by continuing their own lines of enquiry and the findings presented at a class or school conference. Alternatively, arrange an exhibition about all the experiments done.

86: Bicycle

Purpose
To explore many scientific phenomena and principles using the bicycle as a starting point.

Resources
Bicycles and accessories; bicycle catalogues and manuals.

The task in action
Let the children choose some aspect of the bicycle to study. Here are some starter suggestions:

- wheels – tyres, tread, design, road-holding capability
- brakes – operation, efficiency, care
- gears – how they work
- protective clothing – helmets, knee pads, waterproofs, their use and effectiveness
- road safety
- lights and reflectors – how they work, improving their effectiveness.

The copymaster has a detailed diagram of a bicycle on it to help the children's discussion and enquiries.

Teacher help and information
Many children are bicycle owners and this investigation may help them to keep their bicycles road-worthy and avoid accidents.

Connections and extensions
Link this work to the whole school investigation 89: Play safe and to other work on gears and friction.

The work could be extended to other means of transport and of propulsion.

87: Conservation/Pollution

Purpose
To learn about how pollution occurs and how and why it should be prevented.

Resources
These will depend on the children's choice of study but should include, for example, reference books about threatened animals, information about water pollution and purity both in seas and rivers, information about recycling, news of litter campaigns and the rules governing disposal of industrial waste.

The task in action
Let the children decide whether their enquiries should be about, for example, one of the following:

- a threatened species
- water purity
- recycling
- litter
- a 'green' school.

The copymaster is for children's writing or notes.

Teacher help and information
Call on local experts to inform the children about how pollution and conservation are important in their community. Keep a press cuttings file for six months and determine trends in issues of interest. Log the pollution items on BBC TV's 'Children's Newsround' and make a file of them. Help the children to compile some 'school rules' which will make for a greener school. To have some first-hand rather than second-hand experience try something like the following:

- local river watch
- litter round the school perimeter campaign
- survey of dog fouling near school (send letters to the local press)
- set up recycling facilities at school for school meals cans, packaging and school paper.

Connections and extensions
The work could be extended by letting the children catalogue the processes involved in recycling, finding out what exactly constitutes pollution and the scale on which pollution issues need to be tackled to have an effect.

88: Cooking

Purpose
To study chemical change through cooking.

Resources
Recipe books and cooking equipment.

The task in action
Let the children cook! From making table jelly and pouring melted chocolate onto a cake to making bread and biscuits, there is no better way to get children to observe and remember chemical change. The project can involve children across the entire ability and age range. Some examples of change to place before the children are:

- the action of yeast on flour (with sugar and water)
- what happens when the starch in custard is cooked
- the action of raising agents in cake making
- the temporary change in chocolate and jelly when heated
- the effect of soaking and cooking on dried foods
- making yoghurt with warm milk and live culture.

The copymaster is a recording sheet with a decorative border on which the children can write notes or take one home to write down one of their family recipes.

Teacher help and information
Cooking is one of the commonest situations where children can easily observe chemical changes, some of which are temporary and some of which are permanent. While observing health and safety regulations let all the children try all the steps in the production of appetising chemical change.

Connections and extensions
To fuel this 'festival of cookery' arrange a charity day when parents can buy the finished cakes and bread. Ask parents for recipes that children can cook well, try them all and compile a school cook book. Notes about the chemistry involved can come at the back.

89: Play Safe

Purpose
To examine some of the scientific ideas and principles behind situations that may be hazardous to humans.

Resources
A vast array of material including leaflets, videos, information from the police and other bodies and children's books.

The task in action

Guided by the age of the children and the appropriateness of the material introduce one or more of the following:

- effects of drugs – smoking, alcohol, glue sniffing
- dangers of electricity (in the home and at school)
- road safety
- river and canal safety
- railway safety
- dangers of heat (hot liquids, naked flames, fumes from burning)
- danger of the sun (viewing it and staying out in it too long).

When you have selected the topic, give the children the facts and discuss the lines of enquiry they wish to pursue. The copymaster is a writing sheet for the children and the margin shapes are for them to draw in danger signs and slogans about their enquiry.

Teacher help and information

Though the children are young, there are many children who put themselves at risk and the aim of the study should be to provide enough information to enable them to avoid danger at all costs.

All these topics need careful handling. For example, many children will come from families where adults smoke and if you have not consulted these adults you need to be wary of what you may say about smokers. Also, there needs to be a balance between encouraging enquiry and tempting children to foolhardiness. For example, the rule is never go on a railway line, for any reason, whether you think it is safe or not.

It may be difficult to see what scientific investigation may come out of all this. Here are some example enquiries:

- drugs – what is a healthy diet? what happens when we take in materials that harm us?
- electricity – what is the difference between a torch and a light we switch on at the wall? what is electricity?
- road safety – what use are reflective armbands? why do drivers sometimes skid on wet roads?
- railway safety – how are electric trains made to go? where is the electricity? how fast do trains go? why is it impossible for a moving train to stop immediately?
- heat – do liquids always 'steam' when they are hot? are all hot liquids the same temperature? what is in the smoke given off when things burn?
- the sun – what makes our skin darken in the sun? what do sunglasses do?

Connections and extensions

If several of these enquiries are attempted the resultant outcomes can be used as a school resource or put on a database.

Weekend science investigations

The investigations that follow are a few suggestions for ones that children may like to do at home, if necessary with the support or help of an adult. The copymasters are intended to be used as instruction sheets. Each gives the child a picture clue, information about what they need and how to 'make things happen'. For the adults, the note in the top right-hand corner gives the part of the National Curriculum Science Programme of Study to which the investigation contributes, and at the bottom of the sheet are some key concepts that the child should meet while doing the investigation.

Note that no mention is made about where to obtain the resources. You may wish to buy things such as plastic mirrors for the children or tell them where they can be purchased.

The investigations are as follows:

- 90: Bottle band
- 91: Shadows
- 92: Dissolving
- 93: Kaleidoscope
- 94: Periscope
- 95: Marble timer.

You may wish to involve the children in some work to do with similar concepts, before sending a copymaster home. You may choose instead to do these investigations in school, where they would, of course, be equally appropriate. If the concept of weekend science proves popular you and your colleagues can add new ideas and supporting instruction sheets to this resource bank. Time is often too short in school to allow children to modify what they are doing to their own satisfaction. It may be that children enjoy doing investigations at home sometimes because they can take their time.

Name _____

LP & LT: Levels 1/2

Extinct creatures

Choose a dinosaur. Find out all you can about it.

Draw and write about your dinosaur.

Talk about why there are now no dinosaurs in the world.

Copymaster 1

Name _____

LP & LT: Levels 1/2

Sorting/classifying creatures

What is an insect? Find out about insects.

Which of these are insects? What groups do the other creatures belong to?

Copymaster 2

Name _____

LP & LT: Levels 1/2

Fruit seed study

Draw the seed patterns you find.

Plant some seeds. Watch them grow.

Copymaster 3

Name _____ LP & LT: Levels 1/2

Healthy food for a day

Draw and name some healthy foods.

Copymaster 4

Habitats for mini-beasts

Put a large stone or a piece of rotting wood in a damp place in the school garden.

After ten days lift the stone carefully and look underneath. Draw what you find.

Copymaster 5

Name _____

LP & LT: Levels 1/2

Family likeness

Draw faces.

Copymaster 6

Name _____

LP & LT/M & P: Levels 1/2

Bread making

Make bread rolls. Use your senses to tell you what happened.

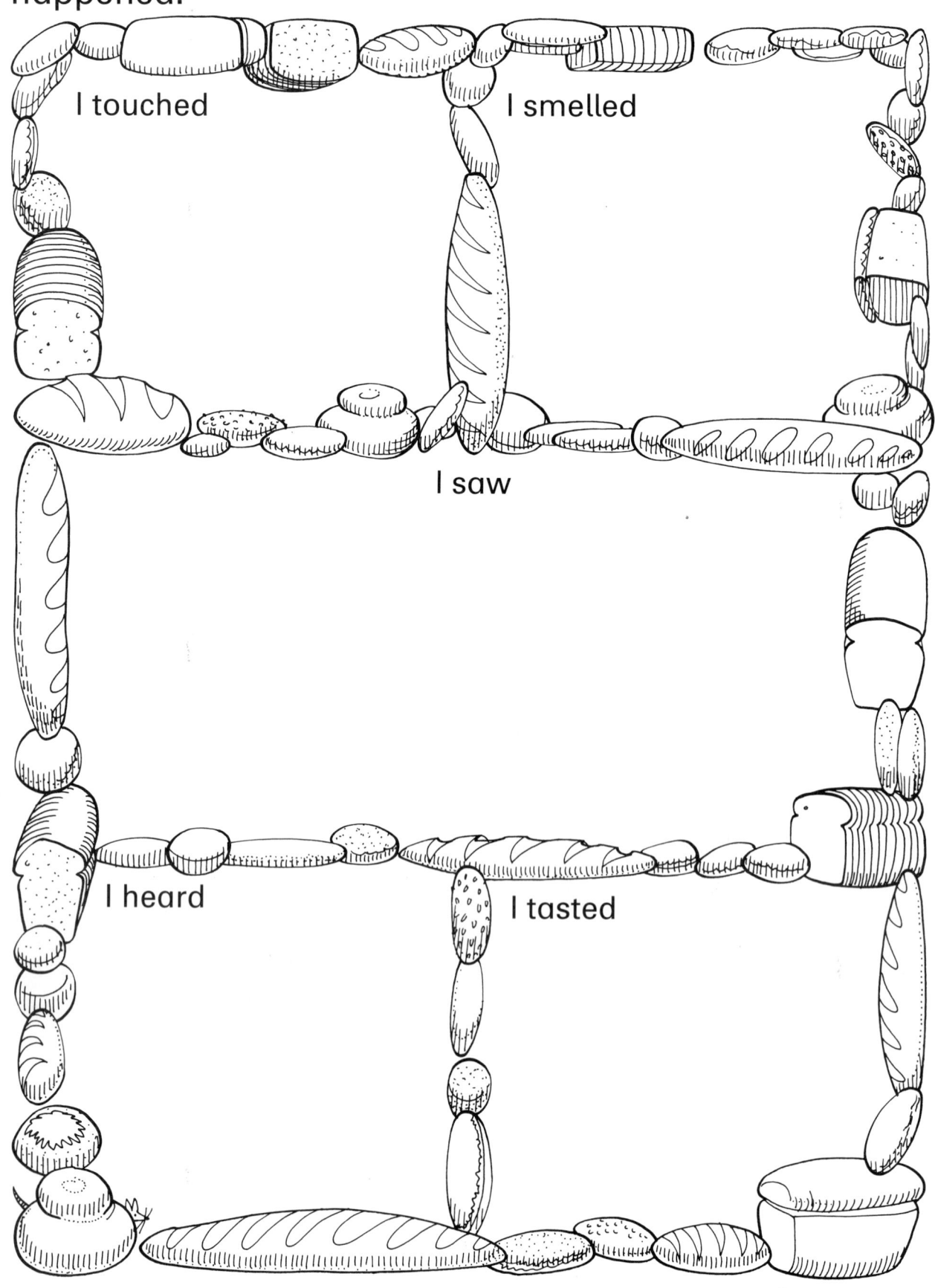

I touched

I smelled

I saw

I heard

I tasted

Copymaster 7

Name _____   LP & LT/M & P: Levels 1/2

Texture and touch

Collect all sorts of things with different textures.

Make a 'feely' picture for a mole.

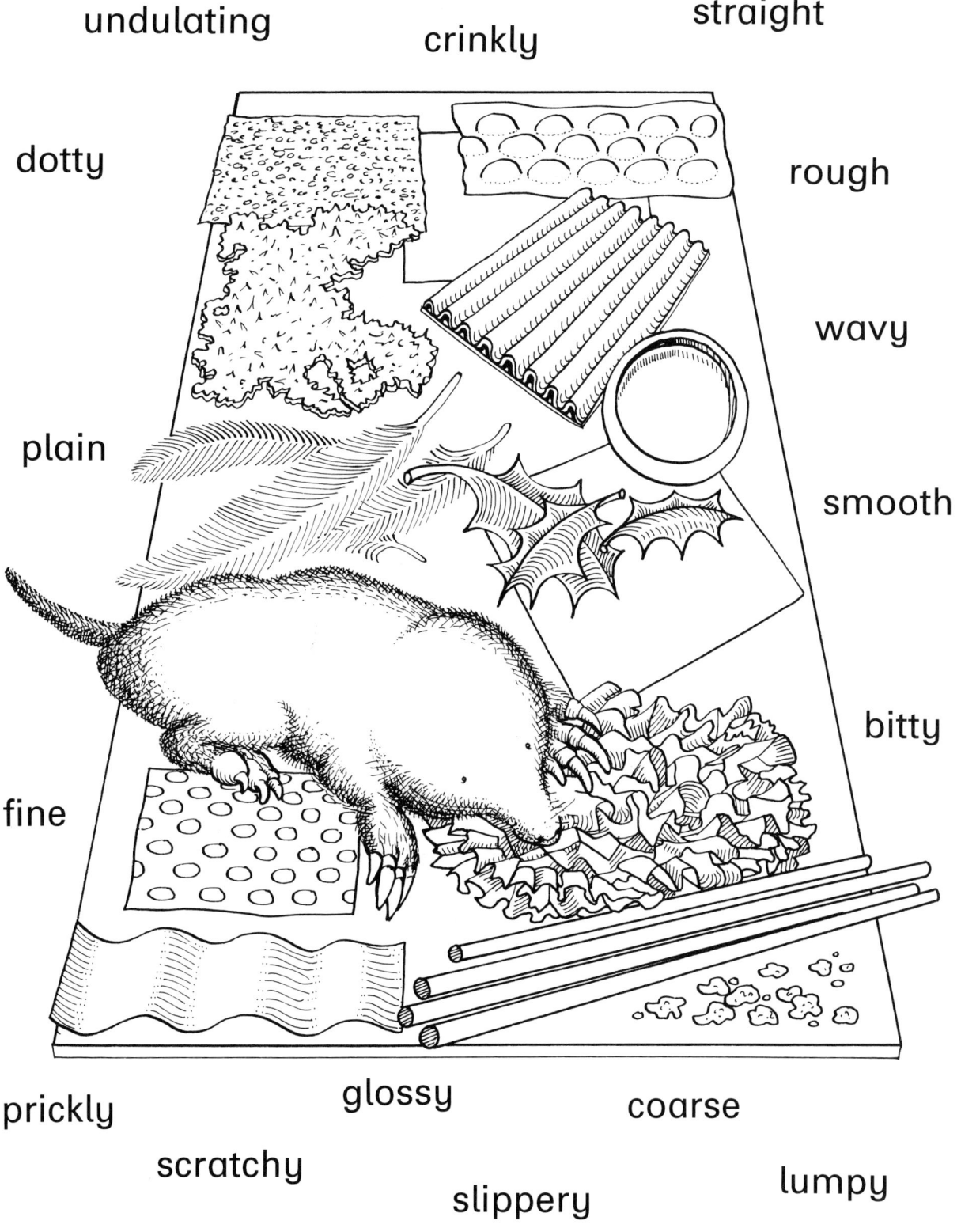

undulating crinkly straight

dotty rough

wavy

plain

smooth

bitty

fine

prickly glossy coarse

scratchy slippery lumpy

Copymaster 8

Name _____   LP & LT/M & P: Levels 1/2

Dyes

What we did:

What happened:

These fabrics take the dye best:

Copymaster 9

Name _____

LP & LT/PP: Levels 1/2

Play telephone

Make a play telephone.

Does it work best with the string or hose straight and taut, or floppy and slack?

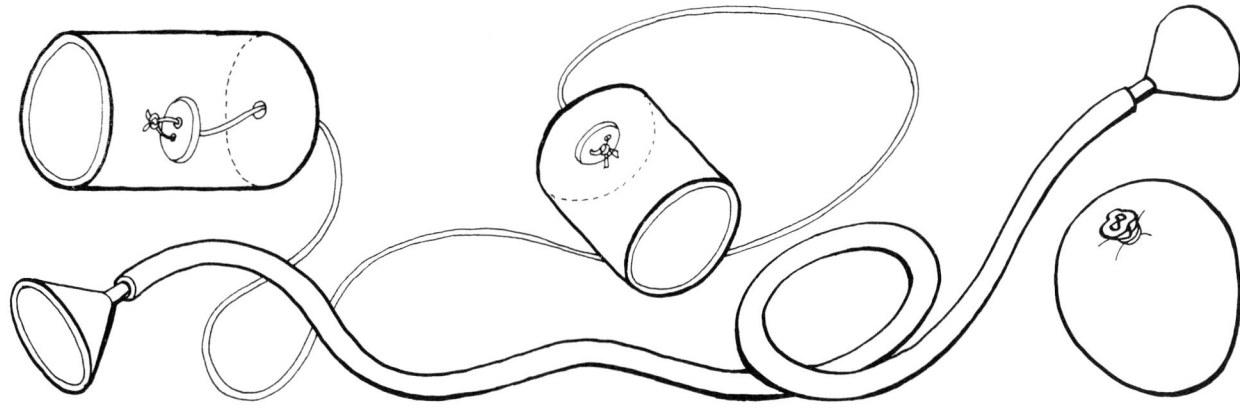

_ _

_ _

Hold a balloon against the tin or funnel while your partner speaks at the other end of the 'line'. Press the balloon on your forehead. Can you feel the sounds?

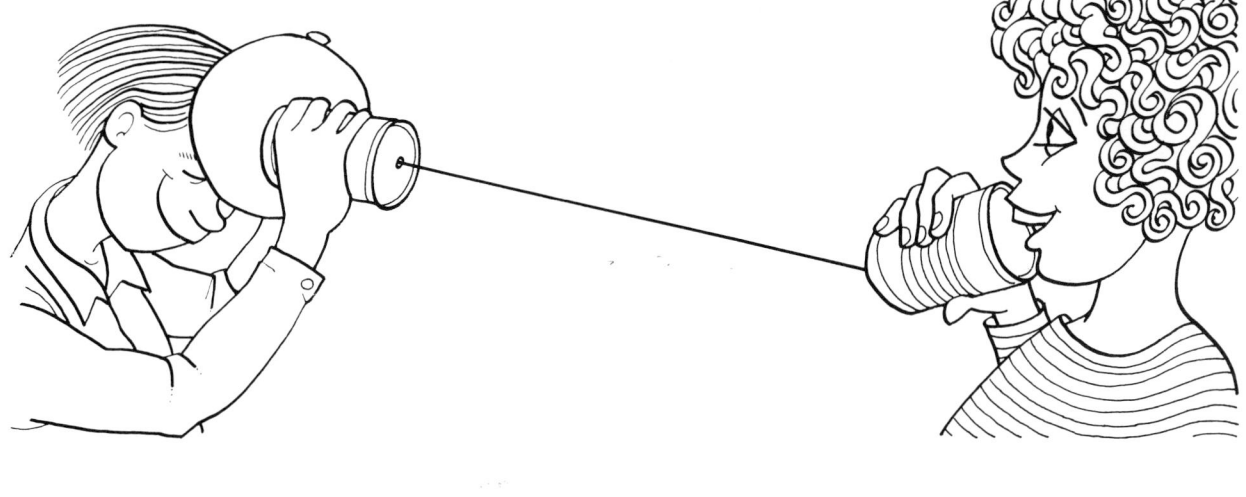

_ _

_ _

Copymaster 10

Name _____

LP & LT/M & P: Levels 1/2

Seeing through

Make a collection of objects. Draw them in the right set.

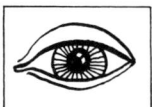 I can see right through these.

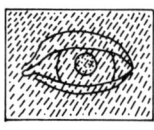 I can partly see through these.

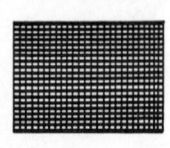 I cannot see through these at all.

Copymaster 11

Name _____

M & P: Levels 1/2

Secret writing

Write a secret message with lemon juice.

Copymaster 12

Name _____

M & P: Levels 1/2

Mixing paints

Mix colours of paint.

Make a colour mix card.

Mix	and	to make

Copymaster 13

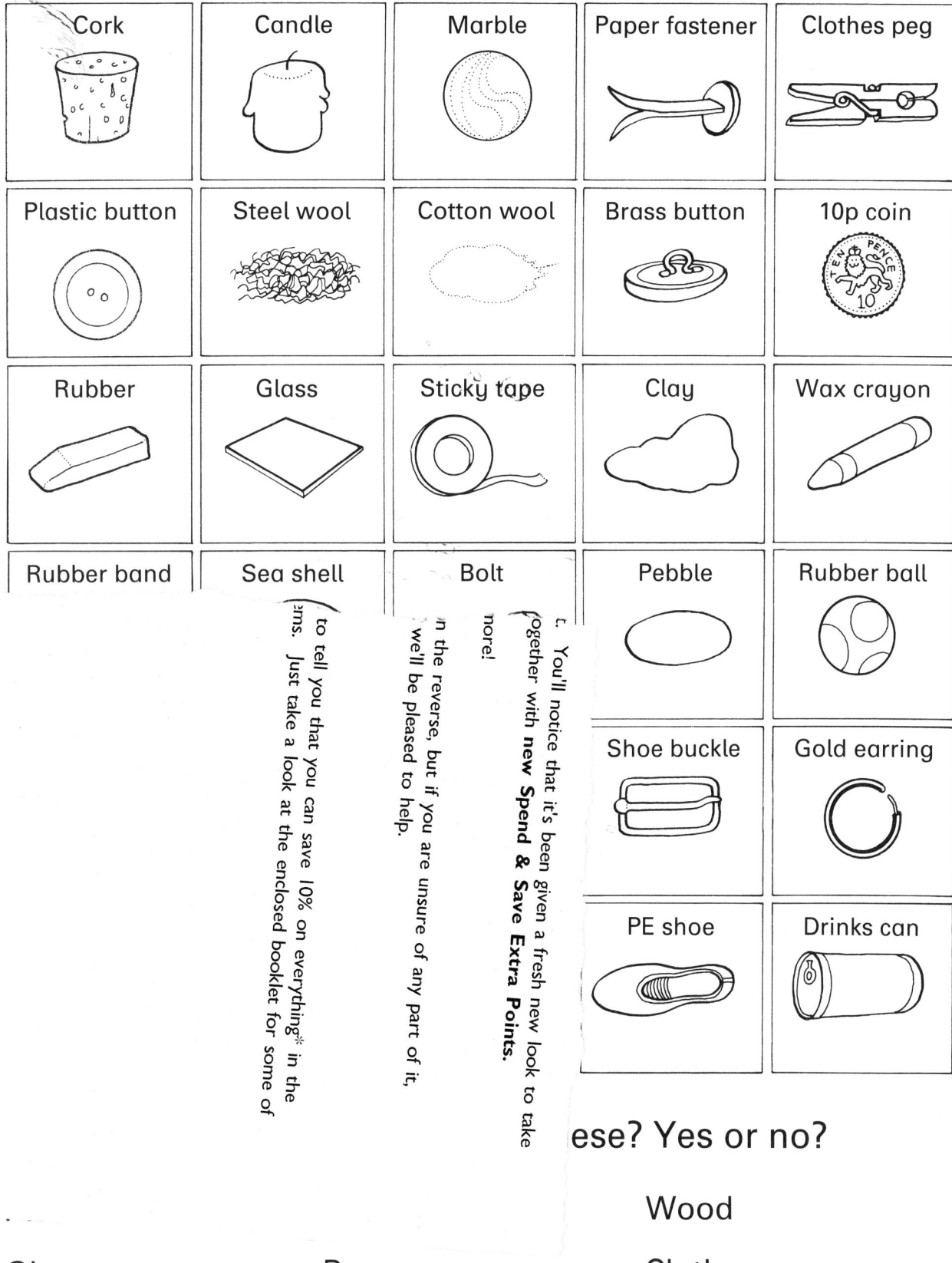

Name _____

PP: Levels 1/2

Mixing colours of light

Colour and cut out to make spinners.

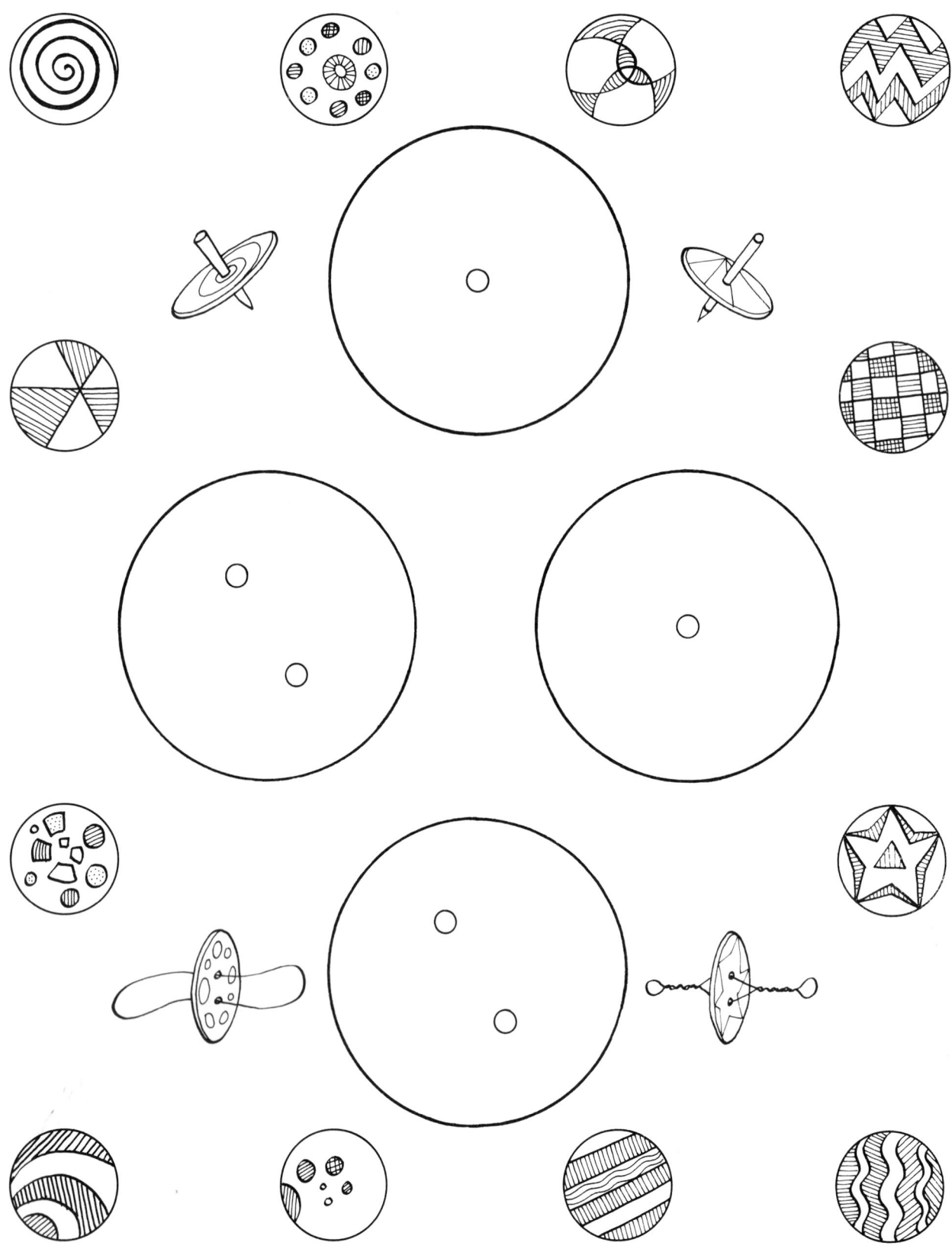

Photocopy onto thin card.

Copymaster 15

Name _____

PP: Levels 1/2

Race around the park

Pond

Woods

Swimming pool

Flower beds

Swings and roundabout

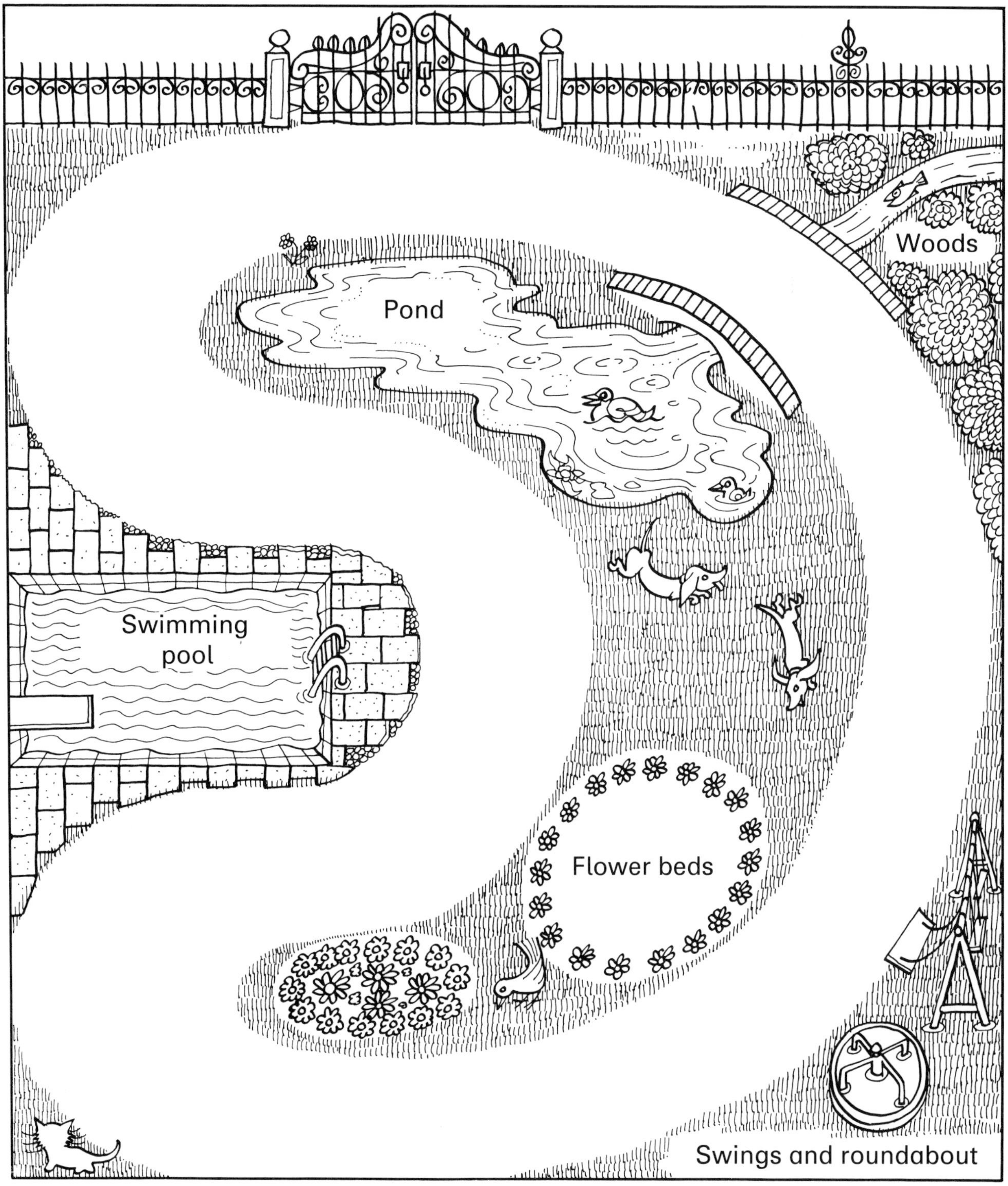

Position magnet here. →

Position magnet here. →

glue and stick | glue and stick

Photocopy onto thin card.

Copymaster 16

Name _____   PP: Levels 1/2

Spinning snake

Colour and cut out.

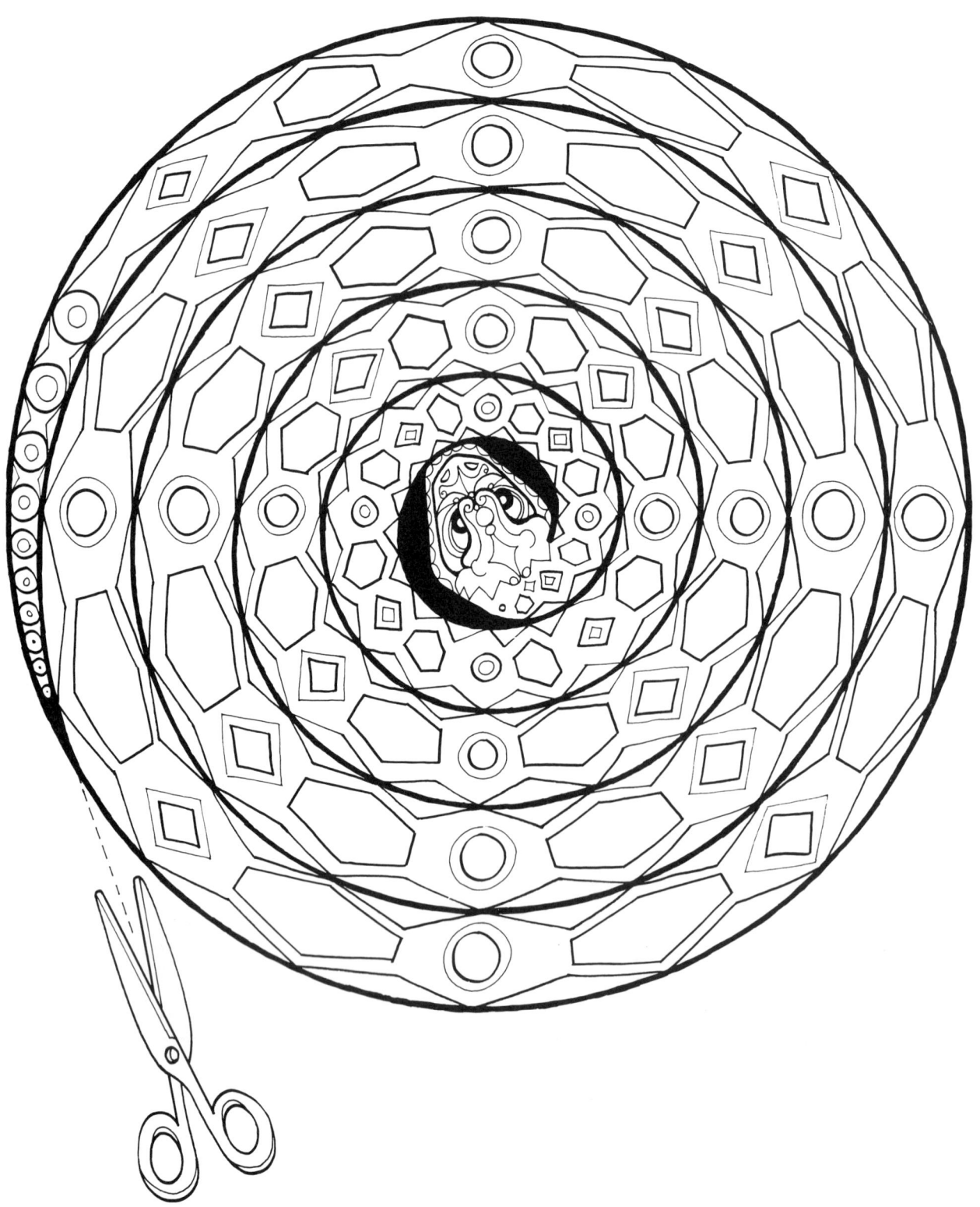

Photocopy onto thin card.

Copymaster 17

Name _____

PP: Levels 1/2

Teddy moves

Get teddy to cross the classroom without your help.

I did not quite do it by

Now I shall try

I did it by

Copymaster 18

Name _____

LP & LT: Levels 3/4

Organic gardening and farming

What is organic gardening? How can you find out about it?

List the ways.

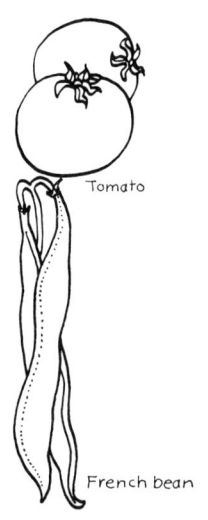

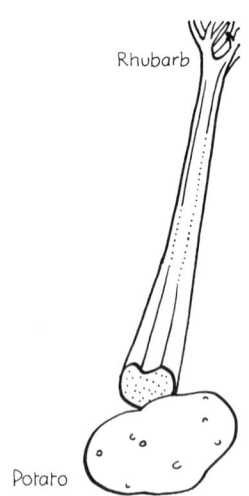

When you know what 'organic' means, buy some organic vegetables and compare them with similar varieties that are not organic. Compare and discuss appearance, texture and taste. Set up an experiment to get ten people's opinions.

Do you prefer organic or 'other' vegetables, and why?

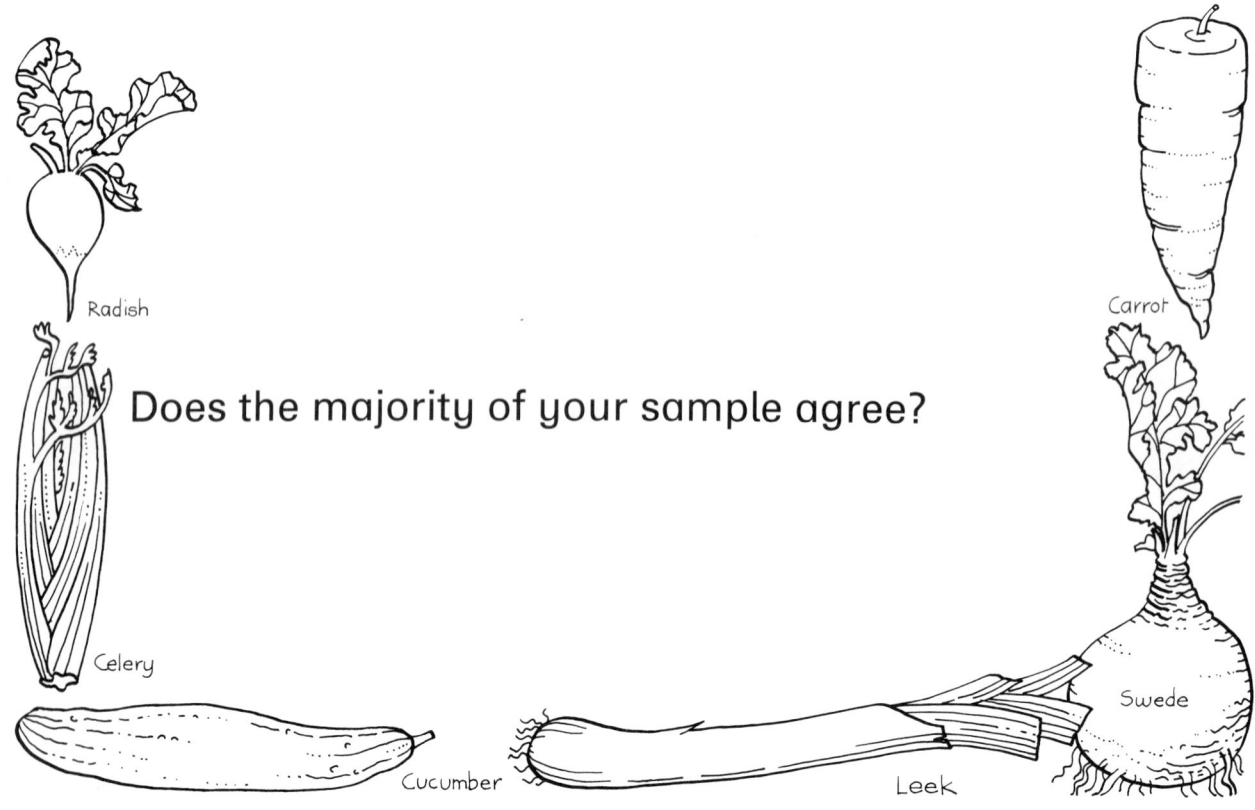

Does the majority of your sample agree?

Copymaster 19

Name _____

LP & LT: Levels 3/4

Food chains

A food chain

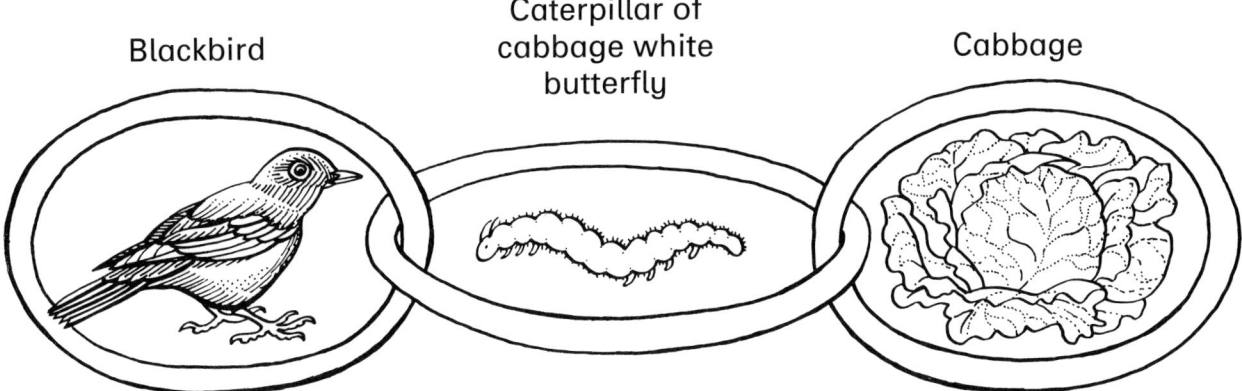

Find and draw some more.

How important are plants?

_____

_____

What happens if one of the creatures in a food chain dies off?

_____

_____

Copymaster 20

Name _____   LP & LT: Levels 3/4

Nutritional value of cereals

Compare the claims made on six cereal packets.
Rank the cereals. Name the overall 'healthiest'.

Name of cereal	Energy ranking

Name of cereal	Protein ranking

Name of cereal	Sugar ranking

Name of cereal	Fibre ranking

Name of cereal	

Name of cereal	

Copymaster 21

Name _____

LP & LT: Levels 3/4

Pet behaviour

Kind of pet

Notes on behaviour

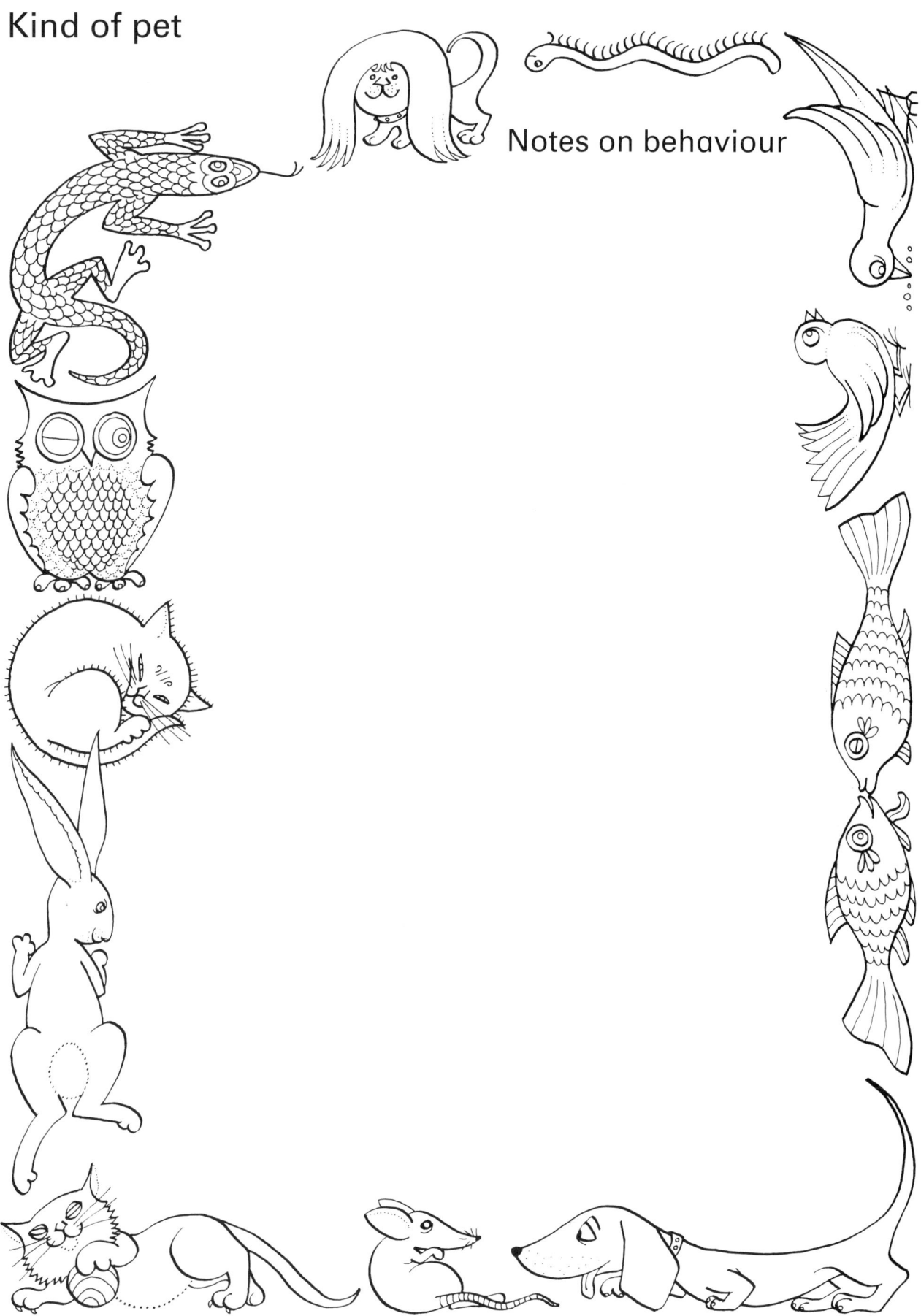

Copymaster 22

Name _____

LP & LT: Levels 3/4

Pet care 1

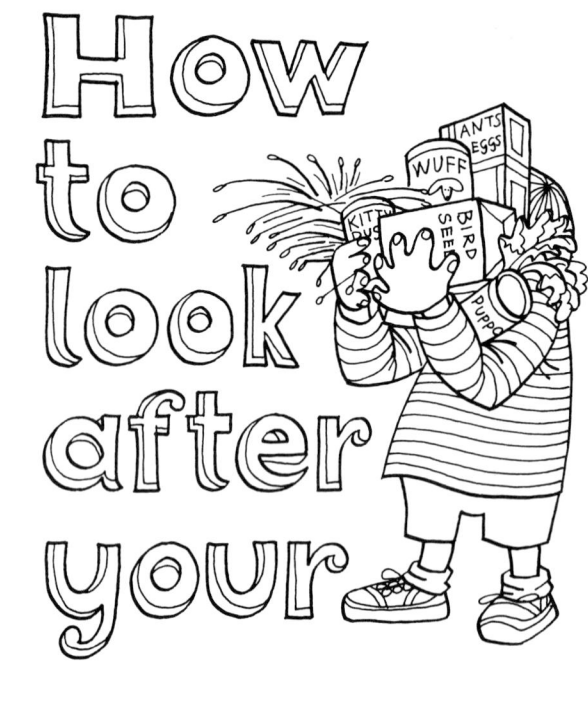

Exercise

Home

Copymaster 23

Name _____

LP & LT: Levels 3/4

Pet care 2

Grooming

Food

Drinks

Copymaster 24

Name _____

LP & LT: Levels 3/4

Seed dispersal 1

Put some fruits on the bird table. Observe which birds eat which fruits.

Write what you observe at the bird table.

Scrape up some bird droppings. 'Plant' them.

Write what happens to the 'planted' droppings.

Can you conclude that birds can help seed dispersal?

Copymaster 25

Name _____

LP & LT: Levels 3/4

Teeth

Look at these sets of teeth. What animals do they belong to and what do you think they eat?

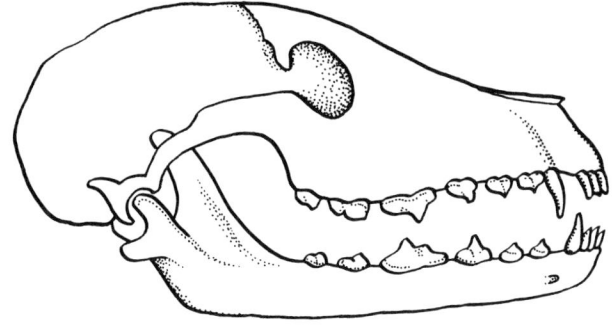

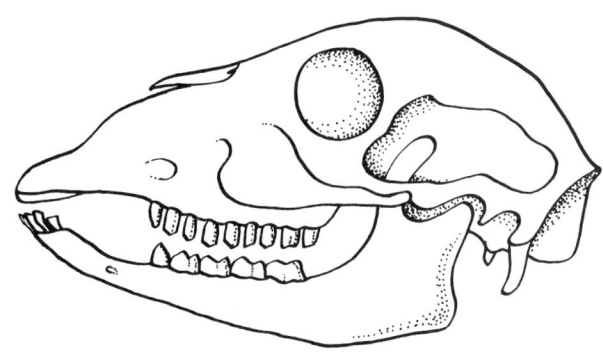

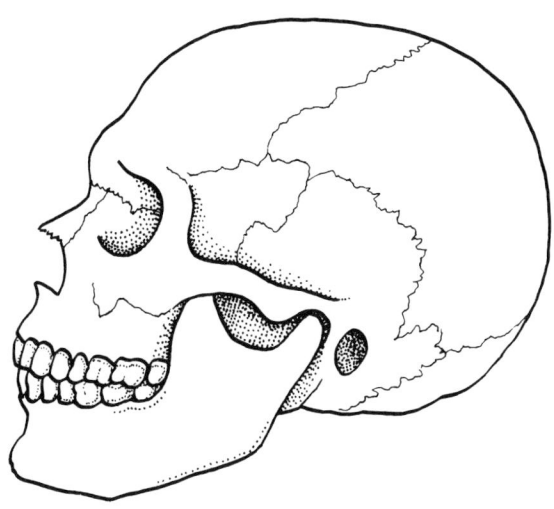

Find out about the teeth of a variety of animals.
Put the information on a database.

Copymaster 26

Name _____

LP & LT: Levels 3/4

Trees

Look at a variety of trees. Draw four different varieties.

Why do trees need leaves?
- -
- -

How can you determine how many leaves there are on a tree?
- -
- -

How can you determine the 'spread' of the branches on a tree?
- -
- -

Why are trees the shapes they are?
- -
- -

Design and make a model tree which satisfies the 'real' tree criteria.

Copymaster 27

Name _____

PP: Levels 3/4

Camouflage

Find out about animals and camouflage.

Make a contrasting display.

Copymaster 28

Name _____

LP & LT/PP: Levels 3/4

Hearing

Choose three sounds you can make, for example, drop a paper clip on a tin lid, tap two wooden blocks together or shake maracas.

With a friend, design an experiment to find out how far away you can hear each of these sounds.

Name of listener ....

Sound of:	Maximum distance heard

Copymaster 29

Name _____

LP & LT/PP: Levels 3/4

Photography

Find these parts on your camera

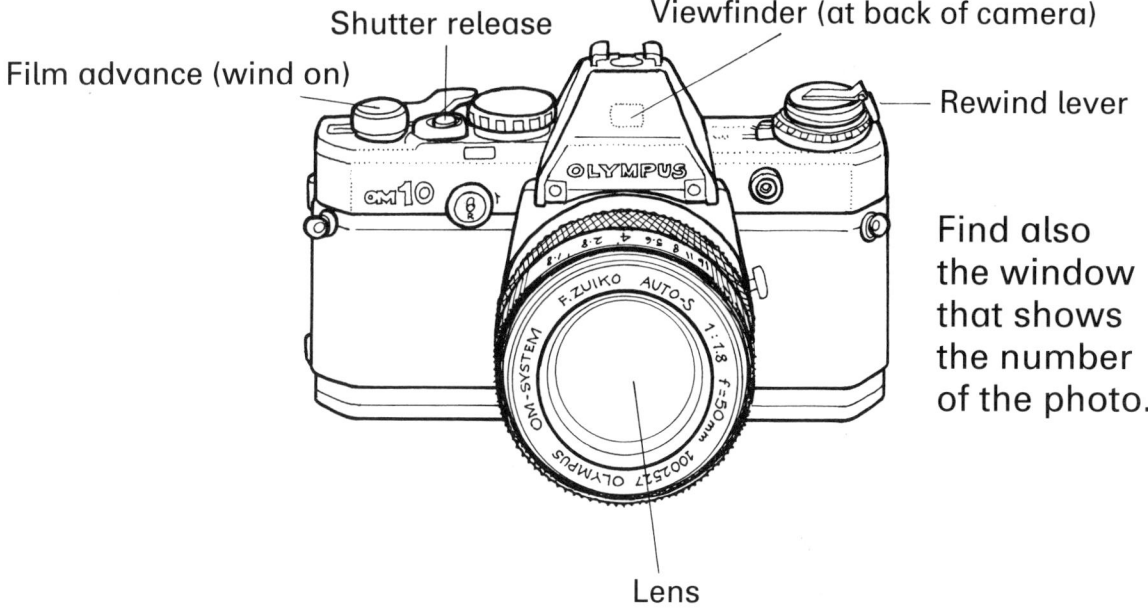

Find also the window that shows the number of the photo.

Talk about and draw what happens inside a camera.

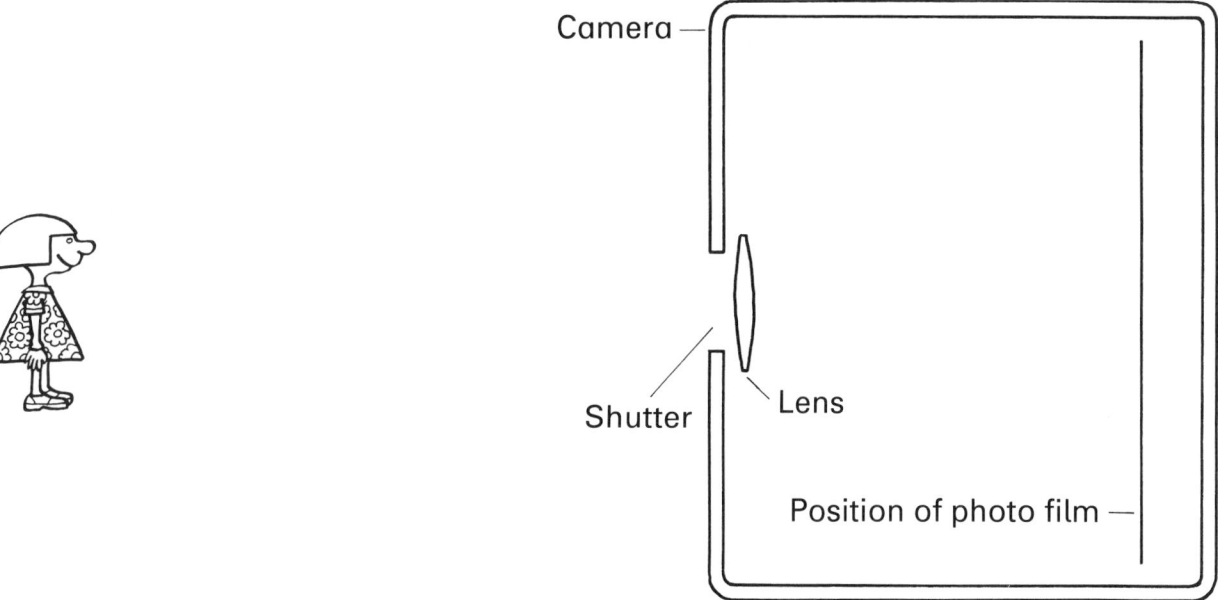

Take some photos around school that show 'change in a school day' or take some photos from unusual angles.

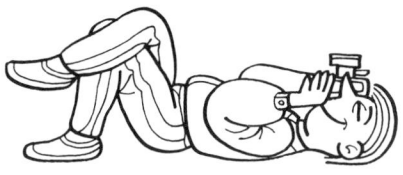

Name _____

LP & LT/PP: Levels 3/4

Seed dispersal 2

Talk about all the ways seeds can be dispersed.
Look at these pictures and try to predict how they are dispersed.
Look up the names of the trees they come from.

Collect some of these fruits. Find out which twist around, which fly slowly, which are lightest. Test out your ideas. Does the size of 'wing' make a difference to flight? Do the lightest fruits go furthest?

Copymaster 31

Name _____

LP & LT/M & P: Levels 3/4

Shoes

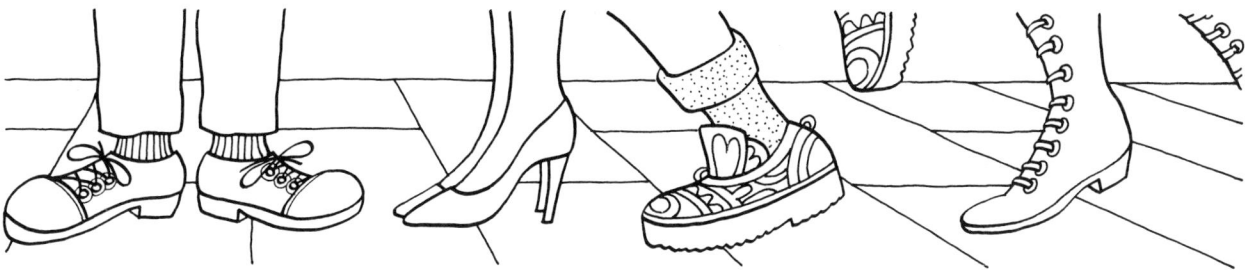

Title

Author

Problem

Collect information about the following:
- range of shoe sizes worn by boys and girls in the class
- difference in length of a shoe from one size to the next
- difference in width from A to G fittings
- styles that are popular with boys and girls.

Design a shoe which is:
- the right shape for a human foot
- popular with boys and girls
- made from environmentally friendly materials.

List the size and fitting range suitable for your class.

Copymaster 32

Name _____   M & P: Levels 3/4

Building materials

Draw a picture map of part of a main street near school. Name the building materials used.

Find out where each building material comes from and whether it is natural or made in a factory.

Find out some of the advantages of two of the building materials.

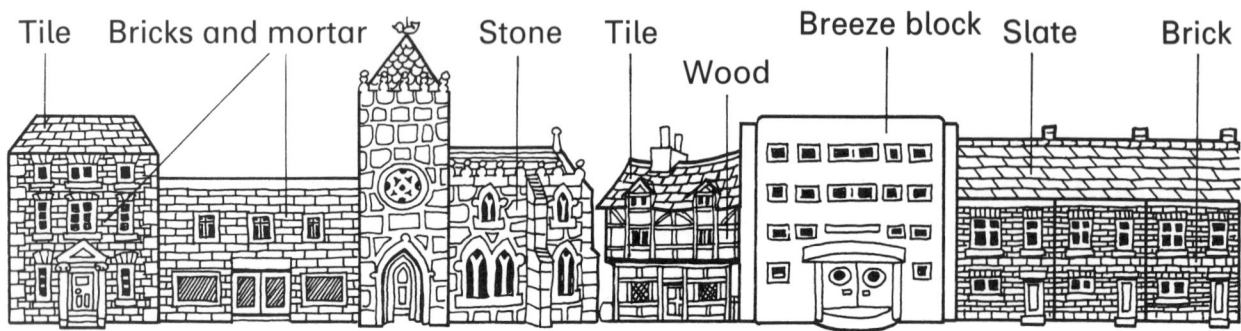

Tile   Bricks and mortar   Stone   Tile   Breeze block   Slate   Brick
                                   Wood

Copymaster 33

Name _____

M & P: Levels 3/4

Crystals

Hang a piece of thread in very strong sugar solution. Leave it for several days. Watch what happens.

Draw what the thread looks like after one week, two weeks, three weeks.

One week	Two weeks	Three weeks

Do the same experiment using salt solution. Hang a variety of things in the solution. You could try a spoon, a thread, a pipe cleaner . . . What happens?

Copymaster 34

Name _____

M & P: Levels 3/4

Drink in the desert

If you were in the desert with these things, and your water bottle was empty, how could you get a drink?

- A long stick
- A few rocks
- A sheet of polythene
- Two pans, a bowl and a cup

Try this experiment in class.

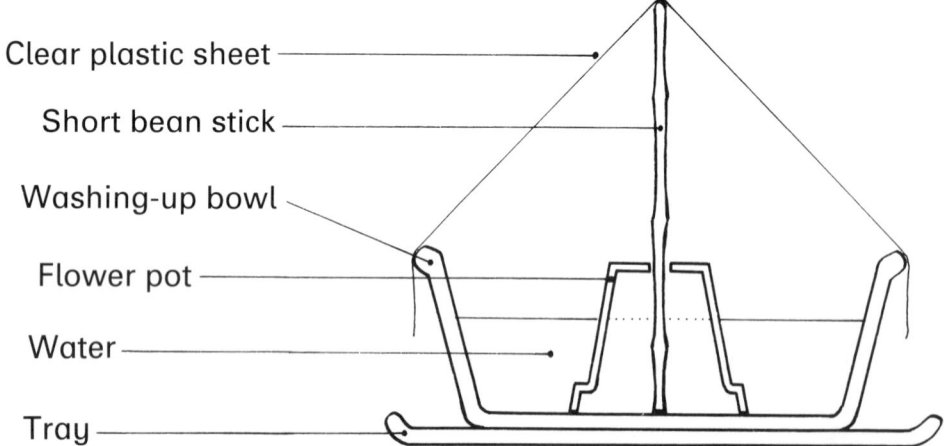

- Clear plastic sheet
- Short bean stick
- Washing-up bowl
- Flower pot
- Water
- Tray

Leave the tray with the bowl on it on the windowsill in direct sunlight. What happens?

Now could you get a drink in the desert?

Copymaster 35

Name _____

M & P: Levels 3/4

Filtering water

Look at a water filter jug. What do we do to use it?

Make a water filter and test it out.
Write about what you did.

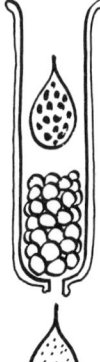

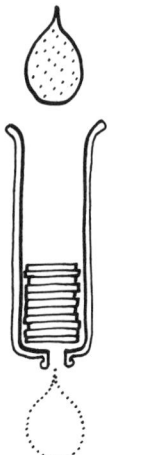
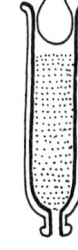
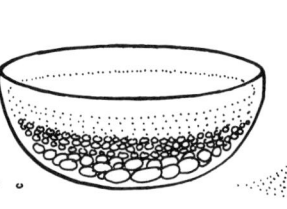

Copymaster 36

Name _____

M & P: Levels 3/4

Swim fabrics

Make a collection of swimsuits. Feel the fabrics.

Find out what the fabrics are made from. Test four suits and find the best.

Draw the four suits and write in the results of your tests.

Copymaster 37

Name _____

M & P: Levels 3/4

Tea making

Test out the idea that tea **must** be made with freshly boiling water, where the bubbles are the size of fish eyes.

Talk about what you need and what you will do. Get a teacher's help with the boiling water.

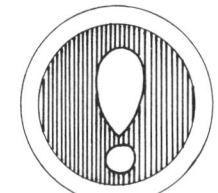

Ask a panel of teachers to be tea testers.

Put your results here:

What conclusion did you reach?

_ _

_ _

_ _

Copymaster 38

Name _____

M & P: Levels 3/4

Temperatures around school

Look around school and find four places which you think will give different air temperature readings.

Set a thermometer at each of these places and record the temperature at four times during a day.

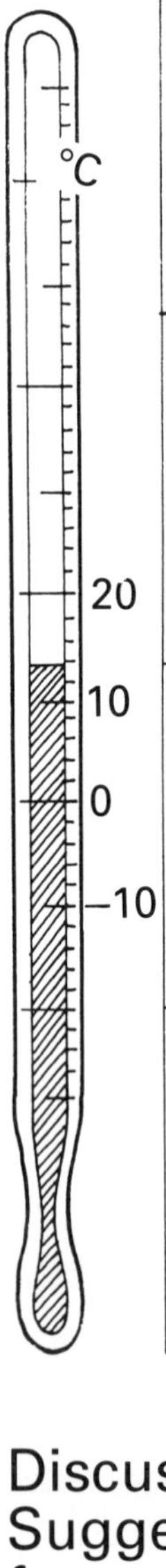

Where thermometer placed	Time of reading	Temperature °C

Discuss your findings. Suggest reasons for any temperature differences and changes and how these should affect what parts of the school are used for.

Copymaster 39

Name _____

M & P: Levels 3/4

Using light-sensitive paper

Put a collection of objects onto a sheet of light-sensitive paper. Lay the paper in the sun for five minutes. Tip the objects off and 'fix' the image that is on the paper. Wash the paper. Allow the paper to dry. Compare the results from the different objects.

Now try again changing either the objects or the time the paper is in the sun.

What I did:

What happened:

Copymaster 40

Name _____

PP: Levels 3/4

Reflective surfaces

Find and draw some things you can see your face in.

Draw what your face looks like in each one.

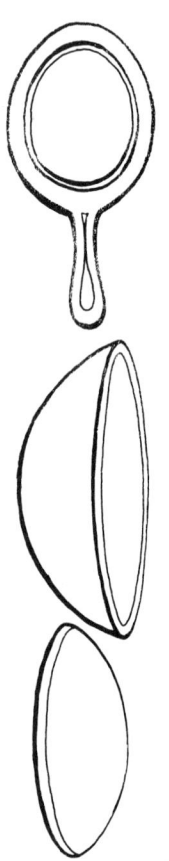

Write down your findings.

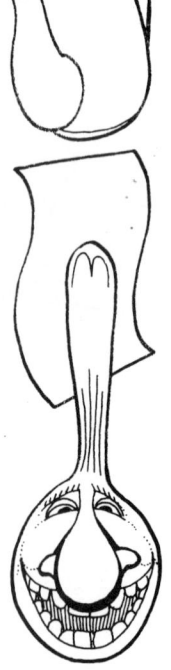

Copymaster 41

Name _____   PP: Levels 3/4

Shadow playing

Make a shadow play screen and puppet.

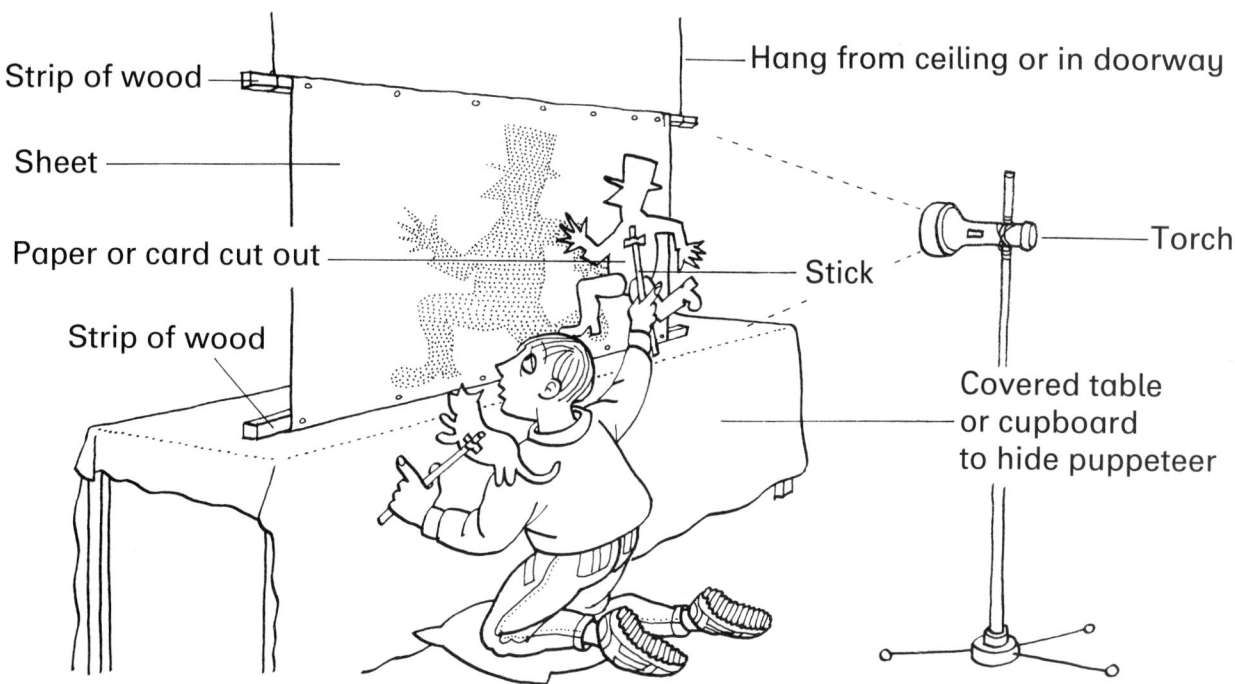

Put on a show. Do some experiments to find out:

How far the torch has to be from the screen to give a 'distinct' shadow.

How far the puppet has to be from the screen to give a 'distinct' shadow.

How shadows can be made larger.

How shadows can be made smaller.

Copymaster 42

Name _____

PP: Levels 3/4

Balloon rocket

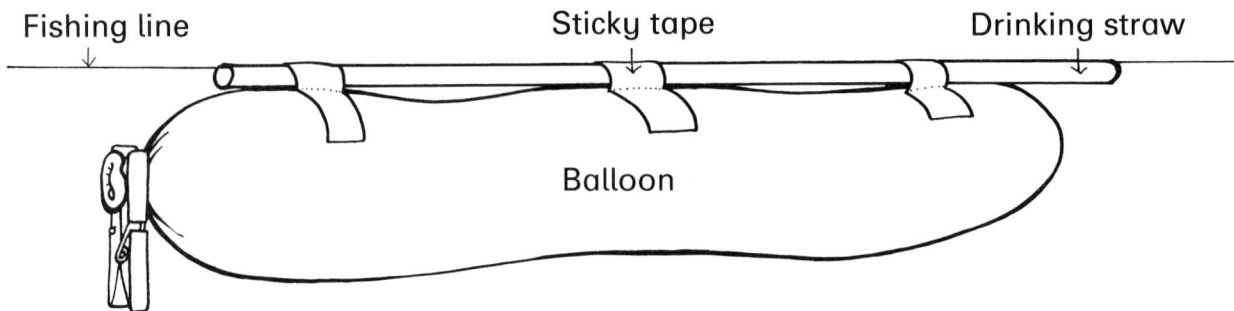

Blow up the balloon and fix a peg on the end.
Stick a straw to the balloon and pass a fishing line through the straw. Attach the line to one side of the room. Hold the other end just taut. Release the peg.

What happens?

Why does it happen?

Will the balloon travel up a slope?

What is the speed of the balloon?

Copymaster 43

Name _____

PP: Levels 3/4

Colour filters

Make a sticky paper picture here using red, yellow and blue shapes.

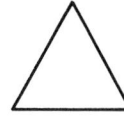

Look at the picture through coloured cellophanes. What colours do you see?

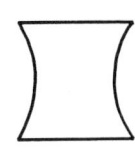

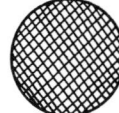

Colour of cellophane	Colour in picture		
	Red	Blue	Yellow
	Through filter	Through filter	Through filter

Copymaster 44

Name _____

PP: Levels 3/4

Cotton reel toy

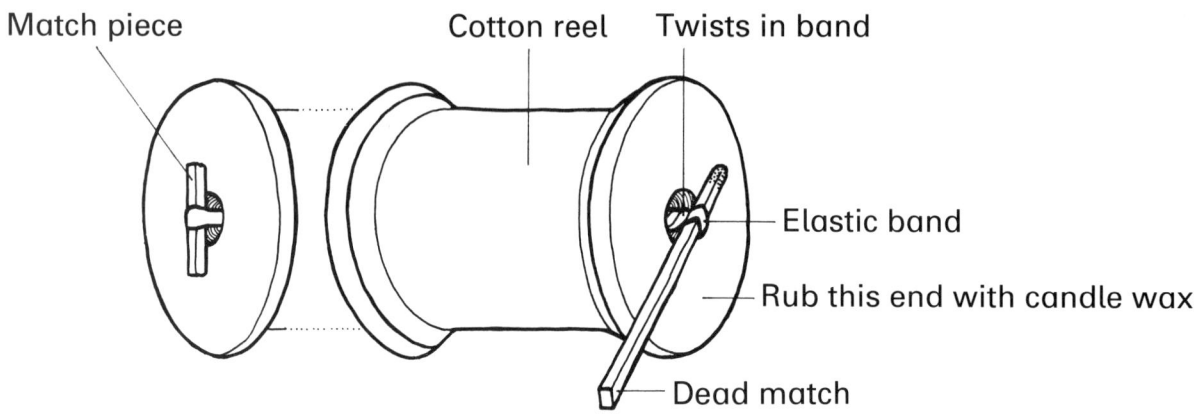

How many turns of the match make the toy move along?

Can you improve the design to make it move better?

Do more turns of the band mean the toy goes further?

Can you make the toy climb a ramp? How?

Copymaster 45

Name _____

PP: Levels 3/4

Friction

Make a collection of shoes which have different soles.

Test how well each holds on a variety of surfaces.
Include dry ground, wet ground, grass and ice.

Make up a scale that goes from 'holds fast' to 'slips easily'.

Find out which kind of sole is best in which conditions.

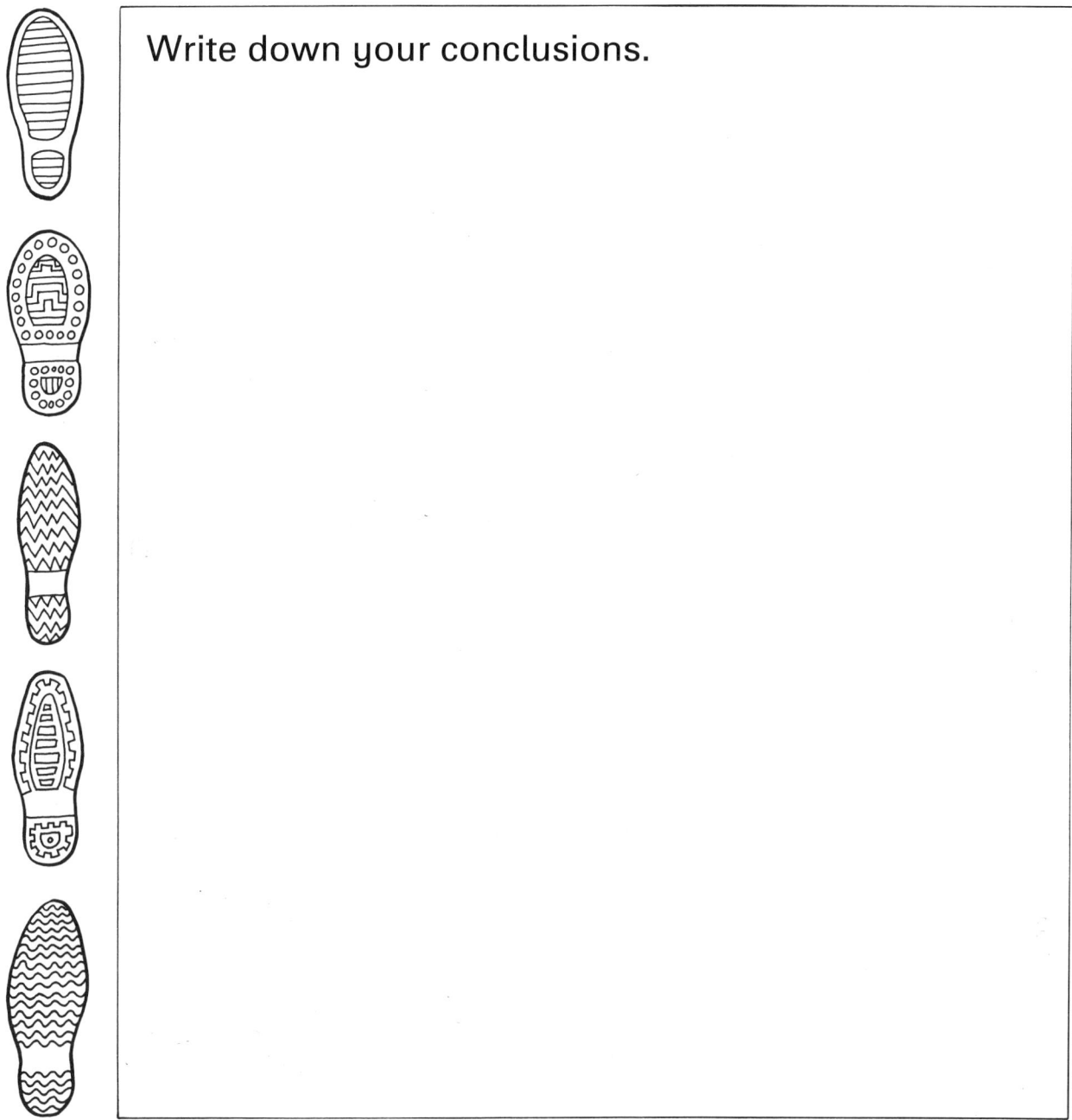

Write down your conclusions.

Find out about the 'road-holding' claims of car tyre makers.

Copymaster 46

Name _____

PP: Levels 3/4

Friction car and trailer

You need: a friction car
a trailer which fixes or ties to the car
cargo.

How far does the car go? Measure the longest distance after three tries.

Car

Car and trailer

Car, trailer and cargo

What cargo allows the car to **just** move?

Copymaster 47

Name _____

PP: Levels 3/4

Good conductors

Connect a battery to two leads and two clips and a light bulb.

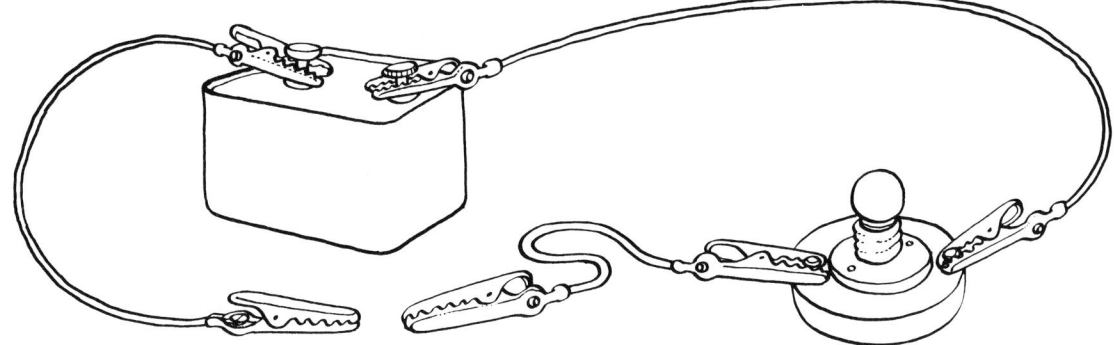

Find some things to put in the circuit, clipped at each end. Which conduct electricity?

These conduct electricity 	These do not conduct electricity

Copymaster 48

Name _____

PP: Levels 3/4

Make a stringed instrument

 ping

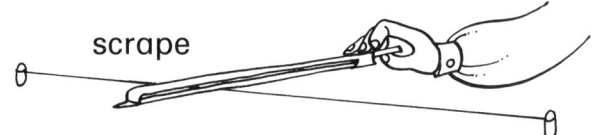 scrape

Make a stringed instrument.

Draw it here.

What happens when you pluck at different places along the string?

How can you change the pitch of the note you get?

Copymaster 49

Name _____

PP: Levels 3/4

Mass and volume

Find three pairs of things which weigh the same but are different shapes and sizes.

Draw the things.

| Pair 1 | Pair 2 | Pair 3 |

Now find three pairs of things of similar shape and size but different 'weight'.

| Pair 1 | Pair 2 | Pair 3 |

Compare the differences in water levels when each thing is immersed (that is the amount of water displaced).

Copymaster 50

Name _____   PP: Levels 3/4

Möbius band

Strip **1**   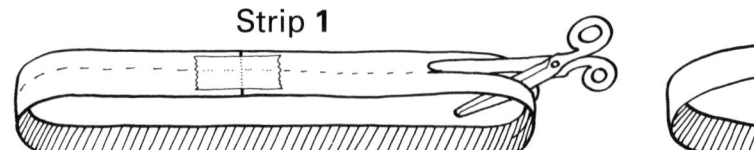   Möbius band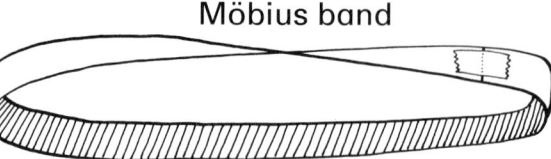

Using 5 mm squared paper cut out three strips, each 28 cm long and 3 cm wide.

Strip 1

Colour one side by rubbing it with a wax crayon. Stick the ends together with sticky tape to make a loop. Now cut the strip along its length. What happens?

Strip 2

Colour one side.

Stick the ends together giving the strip one twist. This is a Möbius band. Now cut the strip along its length. What happens?

Strip 3

Colour one side. Stick the ends together to make a Möbius band. With the scissors, pierce the band 1 cm ($\frac{1}{3}$ in) from one edge. From this hole, cut along the length. You should find you can cut twice around the band. What happens?

Experiment with longer strips to make bands with more twists and wider strips so that you can cut $\frac{1}{4}$ or $\frac{1}{5}$ in from the edge.

Copymaster 51

Name _____

PP: Levels 3/4

Model theatre

Using a shoebox make a scene from a pantomime. Before you stick down the scenery create a circuit with a small bulb which can spotlight part of the 'stage'. Add the characters.

List the instructions for making a model like yours.

Copymaster 52

Name _____

PP: Levels 3/4

Musical instruments

Find out how the sounds are made on each of these instruments.

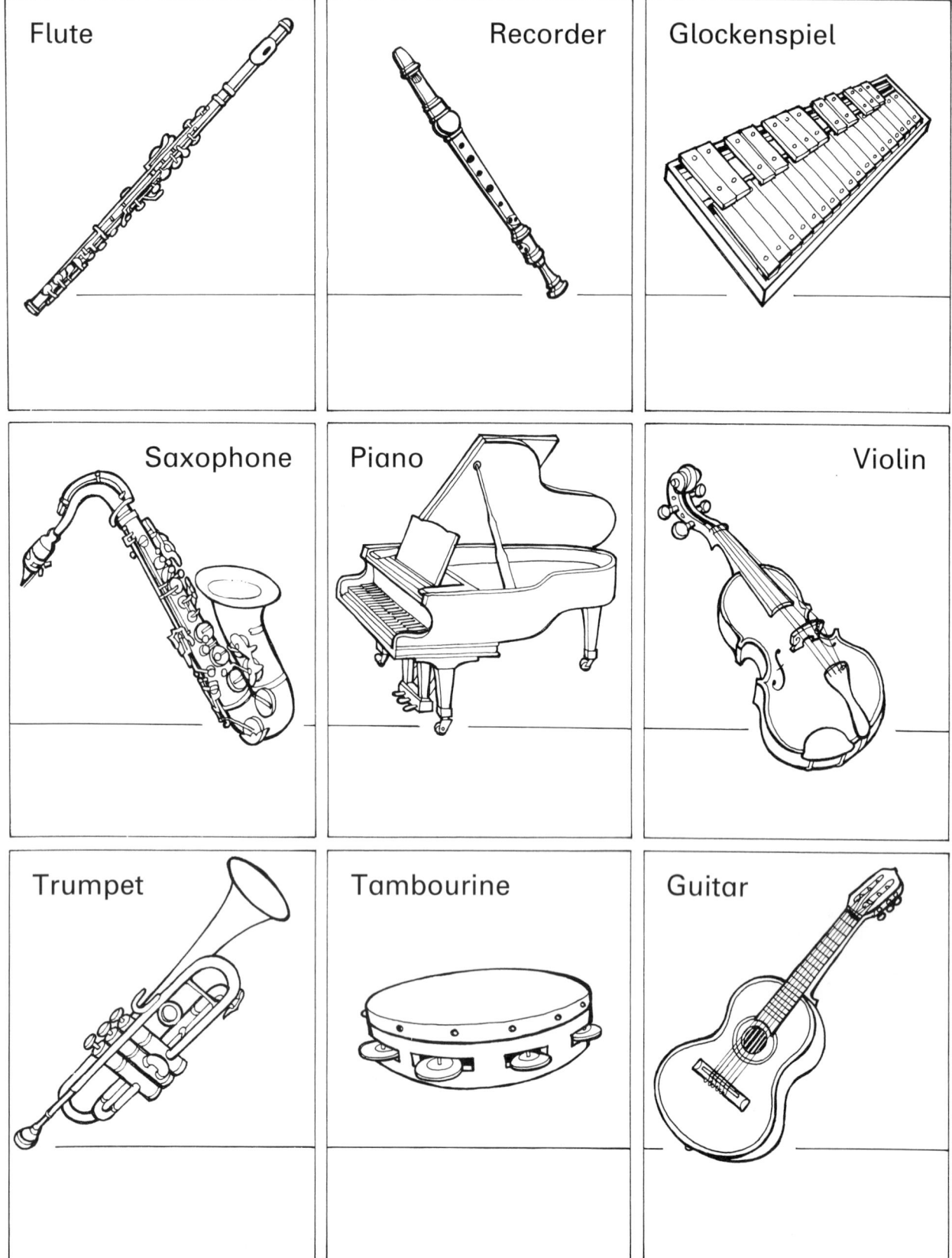

Copymaster 53

Name _____

PP: Levels 3/4

Noises and sound proofing

Visit every part of the school and listen for all the noises you can hear.

List them.

Noise of:	Where heard	Noise of:	Where heard

Invent an experiment to show which materials are good at sound proofing.

Draw up plans to reduce noise in school.

Copymaster 54

Name _____

Optical illusions

How do these illusions work? Find some more.

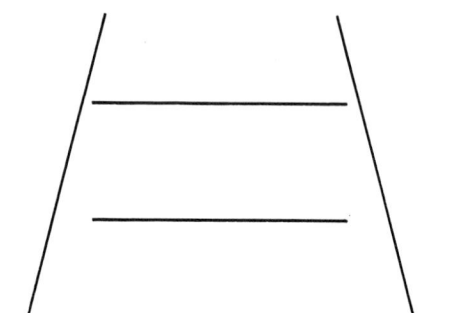

Which horizontal line is longer?

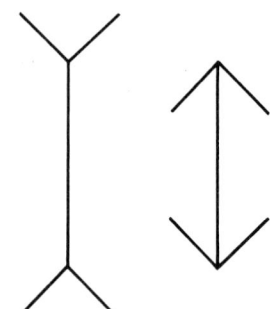

Which vertical line is longer?

Bring your face down onto the paper so that your nose is on the dotted line.

Does the ice cream get into the person's hand?

Cut out the shape below and fold along the dotted line. Glue the circles together. Thread a piece of string through the holes on each side. Twizzle the strings. Watch the frog land on the lily pad.

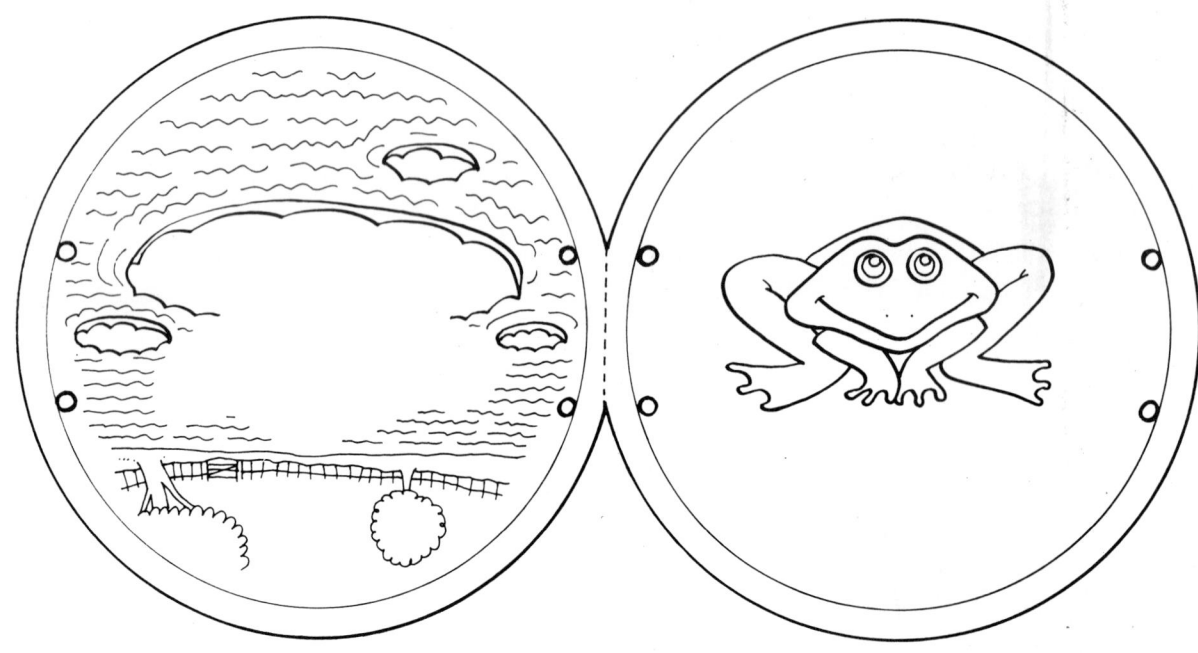

PP: Levels 3/4

Copymaster 55

Name _____

PP: Levels 3/4

Paddle boat

Make a paddle boat.

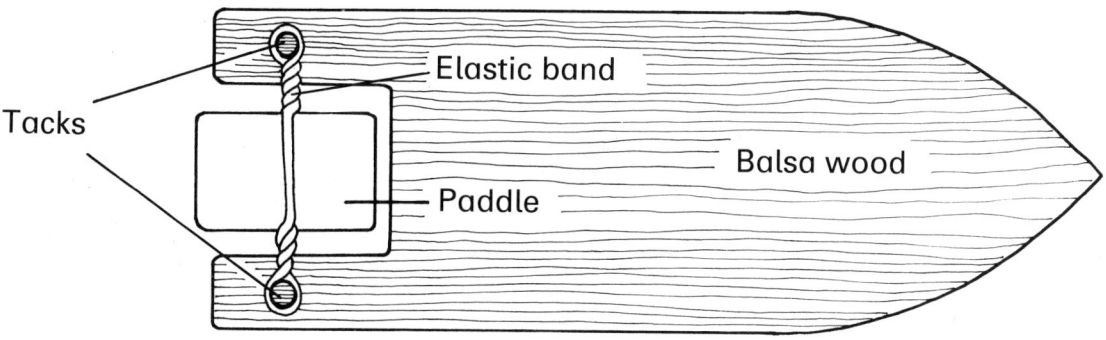

Do more turns make the boat travel further?

Do more turns make the boat travel faster?

Does the size of the paddle make a difference? Test out some different sizes.

What happens when you wind the paddle the other way?

Can you make the boat travel the same distance forwards and then backwards?

How many turns did it take?

Forwards   Backwards

Copymaster 56

Name _____

Paper aeroplanes

Fold a piece of A4 paper

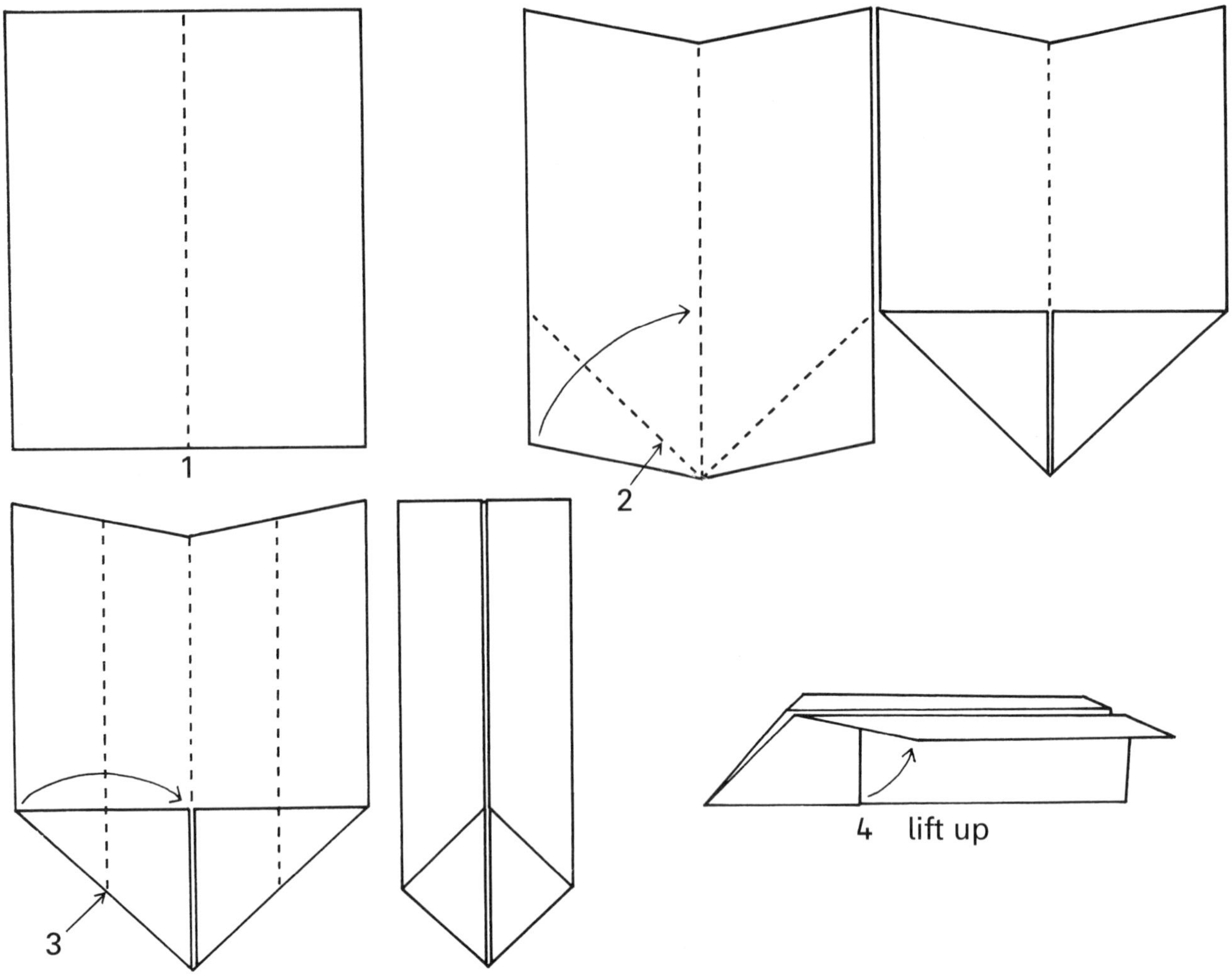

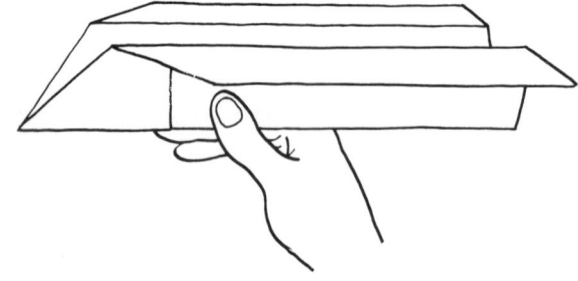

4 lift up

1. Record over five throws the average distance flown.
2. Change the design by folding or cutting to see if you can make the aeroplane travel further.
3. Use paper clips or Plasticine® to see if weighting the plane affects the distance travelled.
4. Write and present a report of your findings.

Copymaster 57

Name _____

PP: Levels 3/4

Poles of a magnet

Find out the direction in which the magnets lie in a pair of magnetic toys.

Draw the toys with the poles in position.

| N | S | N | S |

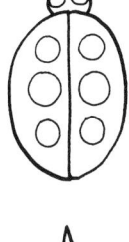 How did you find out the polarity?

Copymaster 58

Name _____

PP: Levels 3/4

Puck game

Trap marbles under jar lids so that the lids move easily around the floor.

Play with the pucks. Draw what happens when two pucks collide, over five trials.

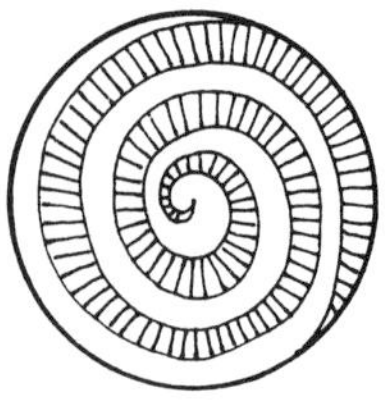

Collision number	What happened
1	
2	
3	
4	
5	

Invent a game using the pucks. Draw the play 'pitch' on the hall floor with chalk. Play the puck game!

Copymaster 59

Name _____

PP: Levels 3/4

Pulleys

Make a pulley.

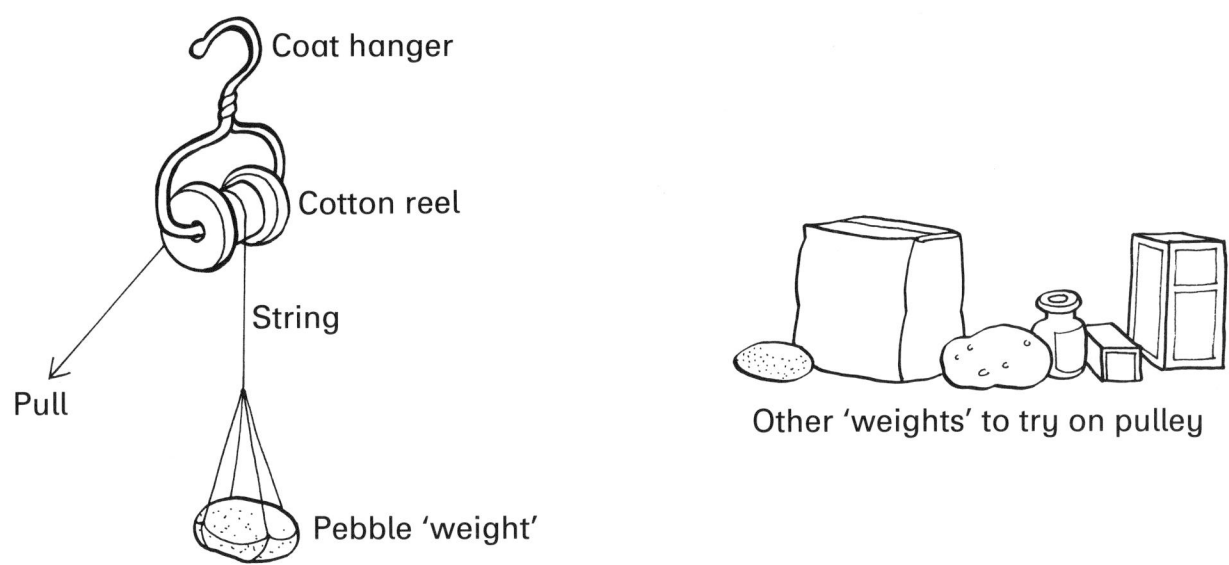

Other 'weights' to try on pulley

Find out how far you have to pull to raise a weight a fixed distance.

Make a complex pulley.

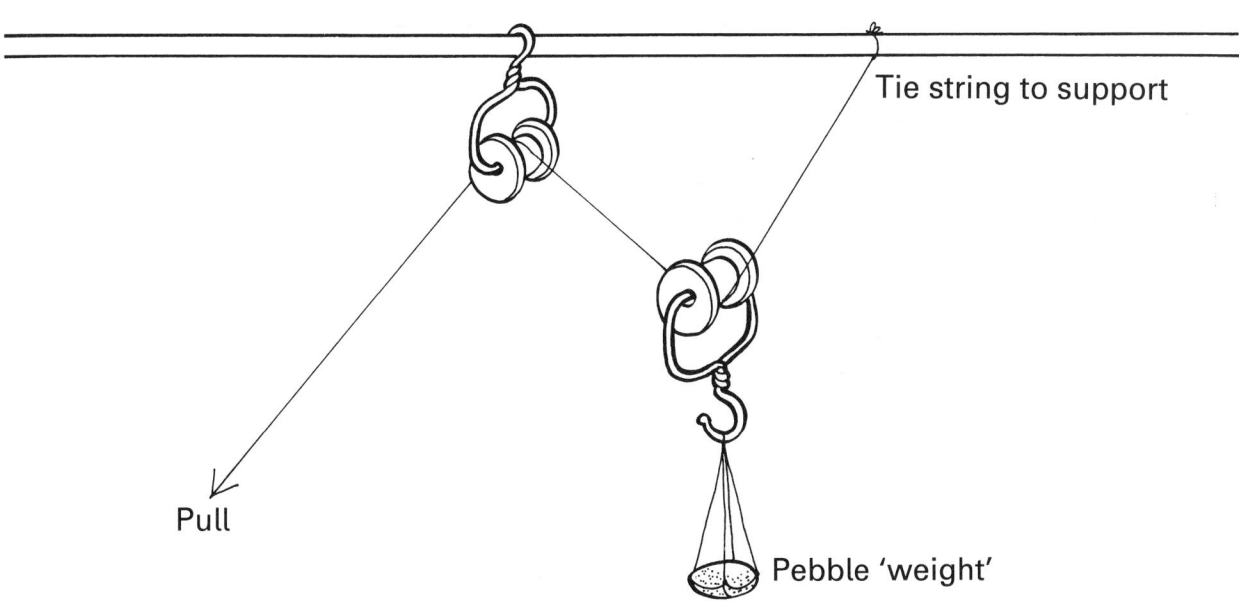

Does this make lifting easier? Use a newton-meter to find out.

Copymaster 60

Name _____   PP: Levels 3/4

Sailing

Make a boat from these.

Margarine tub   Plasticine® blob   Lolly stick

Try out paper sails of different shapes and sizes. Blow on the sail to get the boat to move.

Draw some designs here:

Which sail worked best? Give its shape and measurements.

Why did this sail work best?

Copymaster 61

Name _____

PP: Levels 3/4

Sand clock

Make a sand clock that could be used to measure the length of playtime.

Draw a series of diagrams to show how you made it work and how you improved it.

Copymaster 62

Name _____

PP: Levels 3/4

See-saw

Make a see-saw for some toys.

Bottom part of a plastic bottle stuck to wood to make seat

Piece of wood

Find six toys that will go on the see-saw. Draw them.

1	2	3
4	5	6

Can you get the see-saw to balance? Which toys did you use?

Can you get the see-saw to balance with the heaviest toy on one end and the lightest on the other?
How did you do it?

Copymaster 63

Name _____

PP: Levels 3/4

Signalling – Morse

Make a circuit with a light or buzzer and a switch or easy way of making and breaking the circuit.

Create a code using light flashes or buzzer bleeps. Transmit a message to a partner.

Find out about the invention and use of Morse code.

Send a Morse message using your circuit.

Copymaster 64

Name _____

PP: Levels 3/4

Stopping force

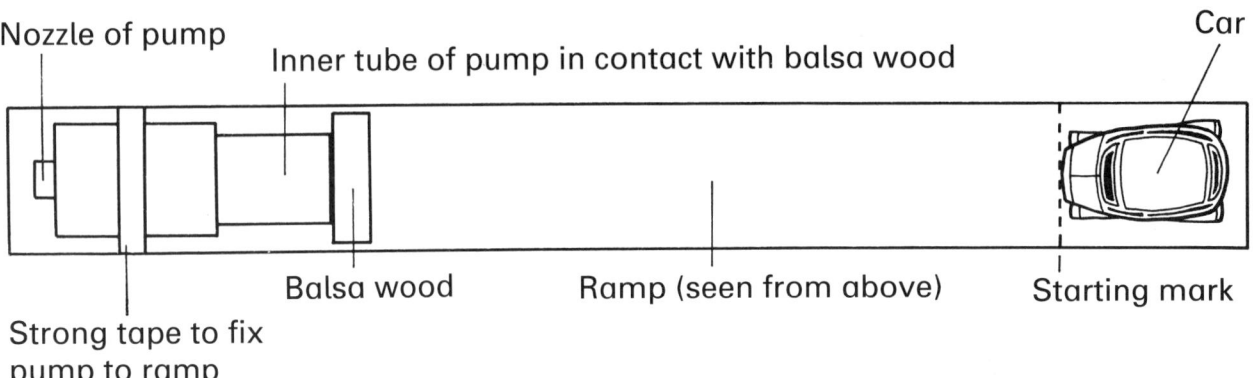

Put each of a collection of toy cars on the ramp in turn. Line each up with the starting mark. Set the balsa wood strip at the same point on the ramp each time. Mark the distance the balloon pump inner tube moves in when each vehicle strikes it.

Vehicle number	Distance pump pushed	Vehicle number	Distance pump pushed

Copymaster 65

Sundials

Collect some pictures of sundials. Find out how a sundial works. Using the pictures design and make a cardboard sundial. Test it out.

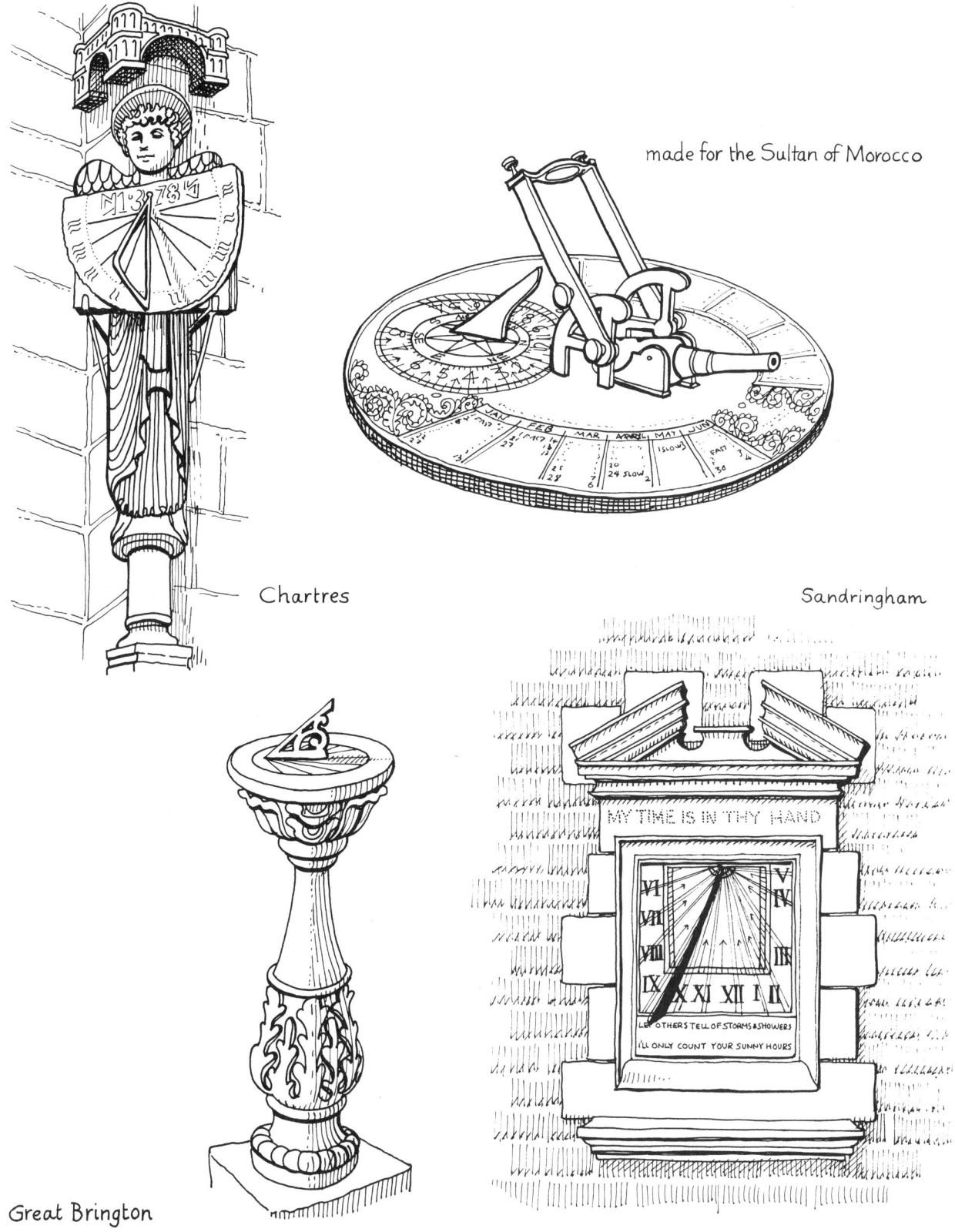

Chartres

made for the Sultan of Morocco

Sandringham

Great Brington

MY TIME IS IN THY HAND

LET OTHERS TELL OF STORMS & SHOWERS
I'LL ONLY COUNT YOUR SUNNY HOURS

Copymaster 66

Name _____

PP: Levels 3/4

Using air pressure

Blow up a balloon until it sits snugly inside a cardboard box without a lid and with one side cut out. Put a clip on the neck of the balloon. Connect the neck of the balloon to one end of a piece of transparent plastic tubing.

Suspend the tubing so that it forms a 'U' bend.

Put some water in the tube so that it part fills the 'U'. Release the clip on the balloon and see what happens.

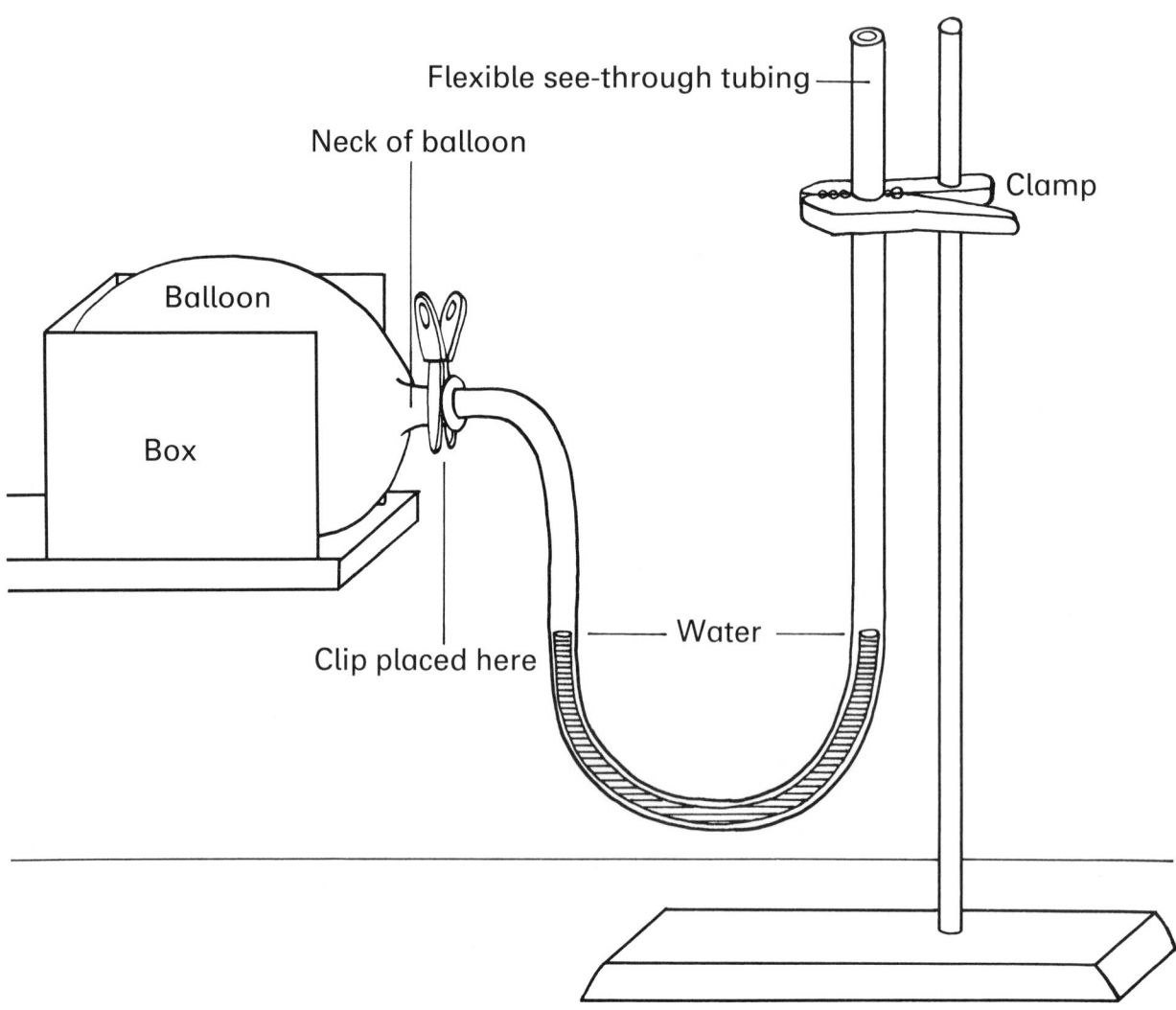

Try comparing the masses of different objects by measuring the movement of the water levels when the objects are rested on the balloon.

Copymaster 67

Name _____

PP: Levels 3/4

Water clock

Make a water clock which can be used to measure seconds or minutes.

Write about the problems you had to solve to get it to work.

Copymaster 68

Name _____

PP: Levels 3/4

Weighing paper

Find the 'weight' of a single sheet of paper. Use any units you like. What did you do?

Copymaster 69

Name _____

PP: Levels 3/4

Wheels

Do wheels have to be round?

Make a truck from a box. Try fitting wheels of different shapes. What happens to the way the truck moves?

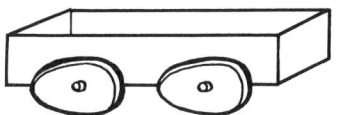 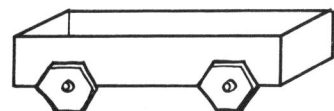

How many wheels are best?

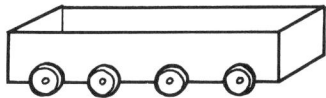 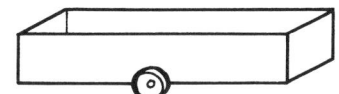 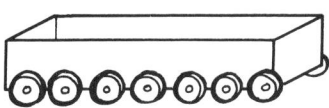

Does the size of the wheels make a difference?

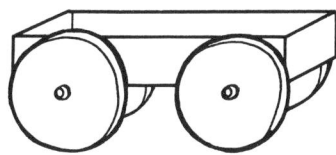 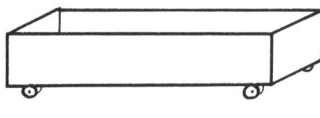

Does it matter where the wheels go?

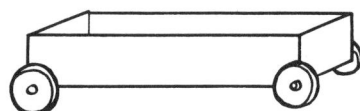 

How can you move a truck without wheels?

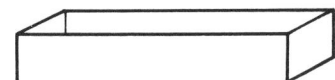

Copymaster 70

Name _____   LP & LT: Level 5

Fingerprints

Get an ink pad.

Make a print of the top part of the first finger on each hand.

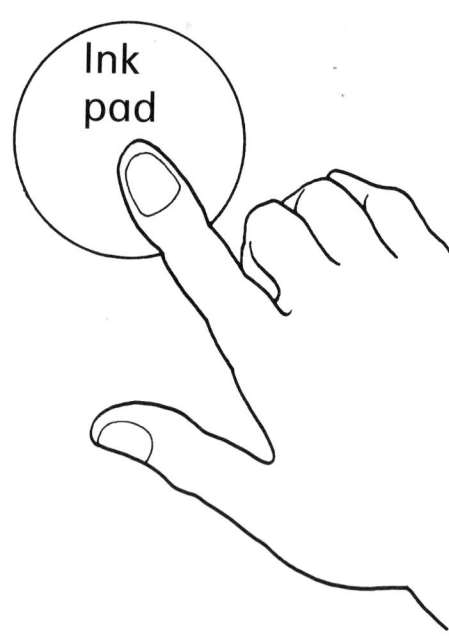

Left   Right

Ask two friends to make fingerprints here.

My friend

Left   Right

My friend

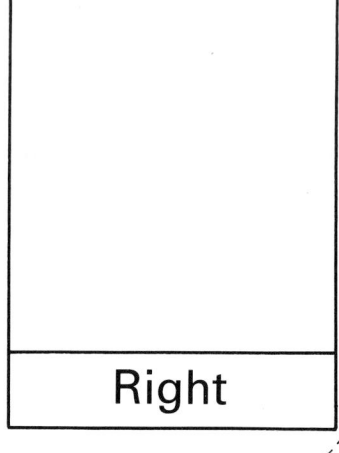

Left   Right

Compare the prints using a magnifier.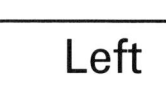

Copymaster 71

Name _____ PP: Level 5

All-weather wear

Look at clothes worn for hill-walking, mountaineering or sailing.

Test fabric samples and fastenings.
Design a jacket suitable for one of these hobbies.
Give reasons for all the choices you make.

List what you tested fabric samples for:

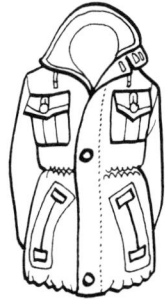

List the issues you discussed about fastenings:

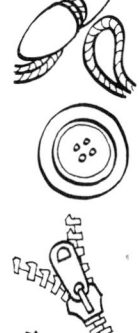

List the important things you put into your design:

Copymaster 72

Name _____

M & P: Level 5

Raindrops

How big is a raindrop?

Let some drops of rain fall on a piece of coloured sugar paper.
Quickly draw round the wet marks the drops make.
Measure some of these across and find the average measurement.

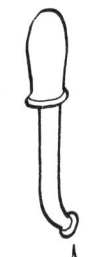

Drip some single drops of water from an eye dropper onto a similar piece of paper.
How do these compare in size with the raindrop marks?

Drip and count the drops of water from the dropper as they fall into a medicine cup or spoon.
Stop when you have exactly 5 ml.

Work out how much water is in one drop from the dropper.
How does this compare with the rain in a raindrop?

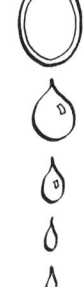

In a light shower, set a bowl of water near the classroom window.
Watch from inside the room while the rain falls.
Count how many drops fall on the water surface in one minute.
Do this for several minutes and find the average. How many drops fell on the playground in one minute? How much water do you think that is?

Invent some more experiments to do with water droplets. For example, does the size of droplet change if you add washing-up liquid, soap or a tea bag to the water?

Copymaster 73

Name _____

M & P/PP: Level 5

Boats

Drop a ball of Plasticine® and a ball of kitchen foil into water. Draw what happens.

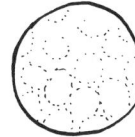

Keep changing the shapes of the foil and Plasticine®. Draw the shapes that float.

Plasticine®	Kitchen foil

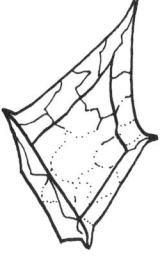

Write an explanation for your results.

Copymaster 74

Name _____

M & P/PP: Level 5

Elasticity of springs

Make a number of springs using wire of different thicknesses.

Wind the wire round a pencil.

Invent a way of hanging the springs up in turn.

Record the starting length of spring and the stretched length, after adding a small 'weight'. Take off the 'weight' and watch the spring return to its starting length. Repeat the experiment adding additional 'weight' each time until the spring does not return to its starting length.

Spring no. and starting length	Weight(s) added	Stretched length	Discussion points/comments

Copymaster 75

Name _____   M & P/PP: Level 5

Electricity and magnetism

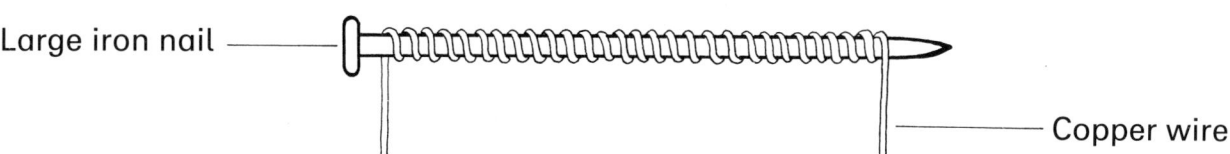
Large iron nail
Copper wire

See if you can make an electromagnet by winding copper wire round a large nail and attaching the ends of the wire to two batteries in series. Add a switch to complete the circuit.

Switch on – the nail becomes a magnet.

How many paper clips (end to end) will it pick up?

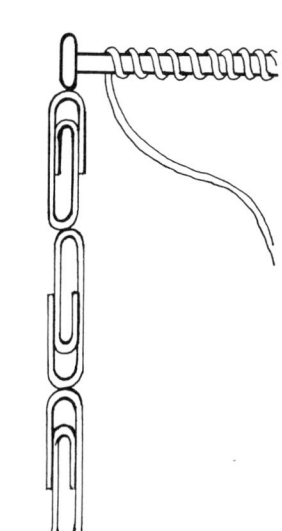

Switch off suddenly. What happens?

Does the number of paper clips it picks up vary if you change the number of times the wire goes around the nail?

What is the heaviest thing the magnetised nail will pick up?

Can you pick up more if you wind the wire round two or more nails?

Copymaster 76

Name _____

PP: Level 5

Hydraulics

Squeeze the water bottle and draw the direction of the water jet each time.

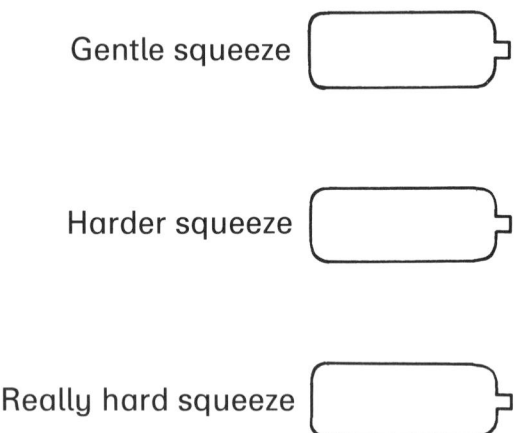

Gentle squeeze

Harder squeeze

Really hard squeeze

Set up this experiment.

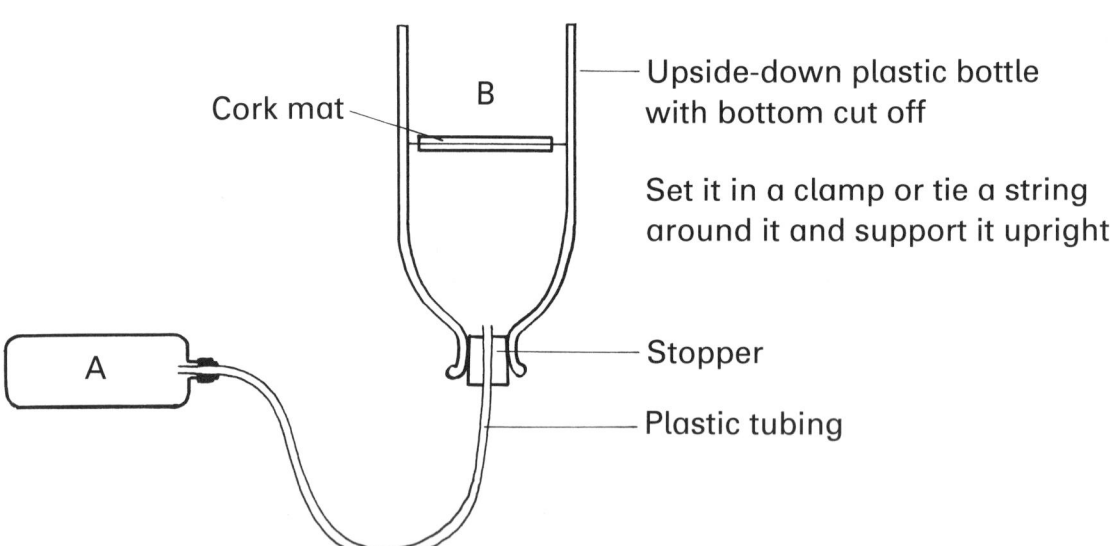

Fill bottle (A) and tubing with water and fill bottle (B) half way with water. Squeeze the water bottle (A). Record what happens to the cork mat. Do several trials, varying the force applied to the water bottle.

Copymaster 77

Name _____

PP: Level 5

Lock gates

Go and look at lock gates. Find out:
– Why the gate hinges are placed where they are.
– Why the gates do not sit straight when closed.
– Where the sluices are and how they operate.
– What the teeth on a winch are like and why.

 Write down what you have found out.

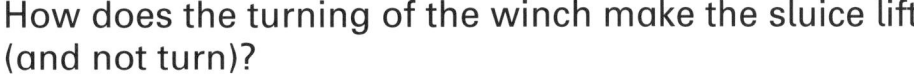 How does the turning of the winch make the sluice lift (and not turn)?

Make models to show how winches and sluices work.

Copymaster 78

Name _____   PP: Level 5

Pelican crossing

Find out the pattern of lights at a Pelican crossing.

Take care.

Draw or write about the pattern for drivers and pedestrians.

How could this pattern be improved so that drivers and pedestrians have warning and so that partially-sighted people can cross safely?

Copymaster 79

Name _____

PP: Level 5

Pendulum

Hang a piece of string from a clamp or cuphook and tie a heavy button or small washer on the end. Set the pendulum swinging. Estimate how many swings in one minute. Now check your estimate over five trials.

Number of swings per minute	Trial 1	Trial 2	Trial 3	Trial 4	Trial 5

Write down your predictions about what would happen to the number of swings per minute if the following experiments are done:

Heavier 'weight'	
Lighter 'weight'	
Longer string	
Shorter string	
Bigger starting arc	
Smaller starting arc	

Devise and carry through experiments to test your predictions. Write your conclusions here:

Copymaster 80

Name _____

PP: Level 5

Signalling – lighthouses

Every lighthouse has its own pattern of flashes. Find out the pattern for a lighthouse as close as possible to your school.

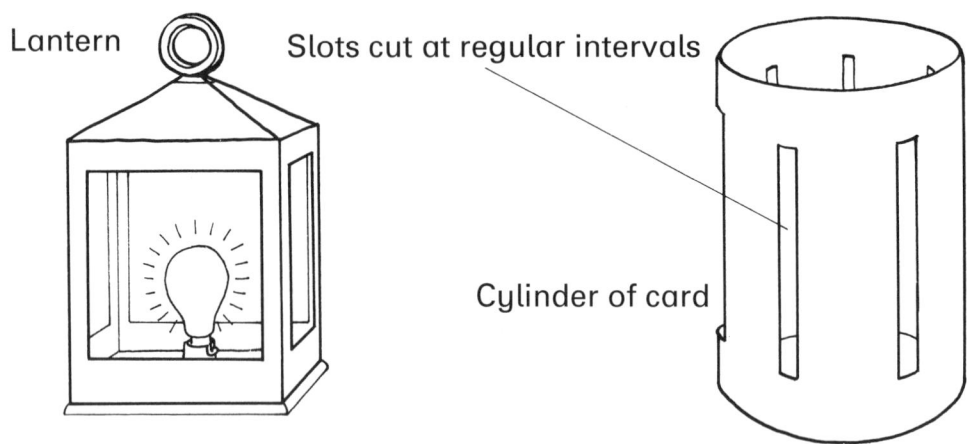

See if you can show how a lighthouse flashes.

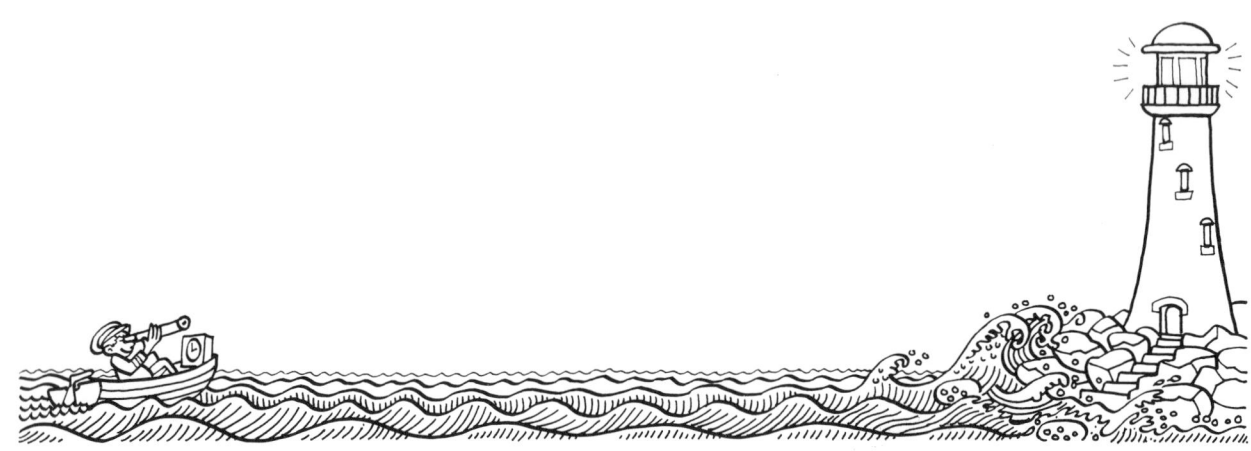

Copymaster 81

PP: Level 5

Skip

Skip with a really long piece of wire which is connected at both ends to a sensitive galvanometer.

What happens? What explanation do you have for what happens?

Copymaster 82

PP: Level 5

Spectrum

Use a strong washing-up liquid solution and a wire hoop to blow bubbles.

What do the bubbles look like?

Partly cover a torch to make a narrow light beam.
Shine the beam through a prism. Try doing this in a darkened room.
What happens?

If you put a second prism in the path of the light what happens?

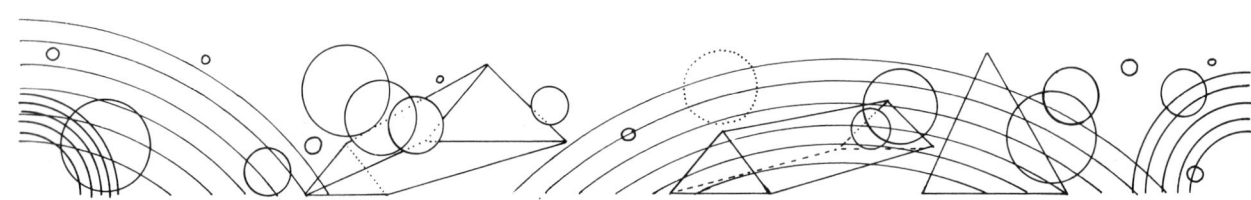

Copymaster 83

Name _____

PP: Level 5

Speed and distance

Find the average distance travelled by a car placed half way up and then at the top of a fixed long ramp.

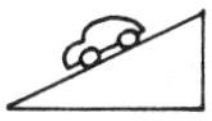 Trial no.	Distance travelled in cm	Discussion points
	Average distance	

 Trial no.	Distance travelled in cm	Discussion points
	Average distance	

Copymaster 84

Name _____ Suitable for all ATs

Science in a rhyme

Copymaster 85

Name _____

Suitable for all ATs

Bicycle

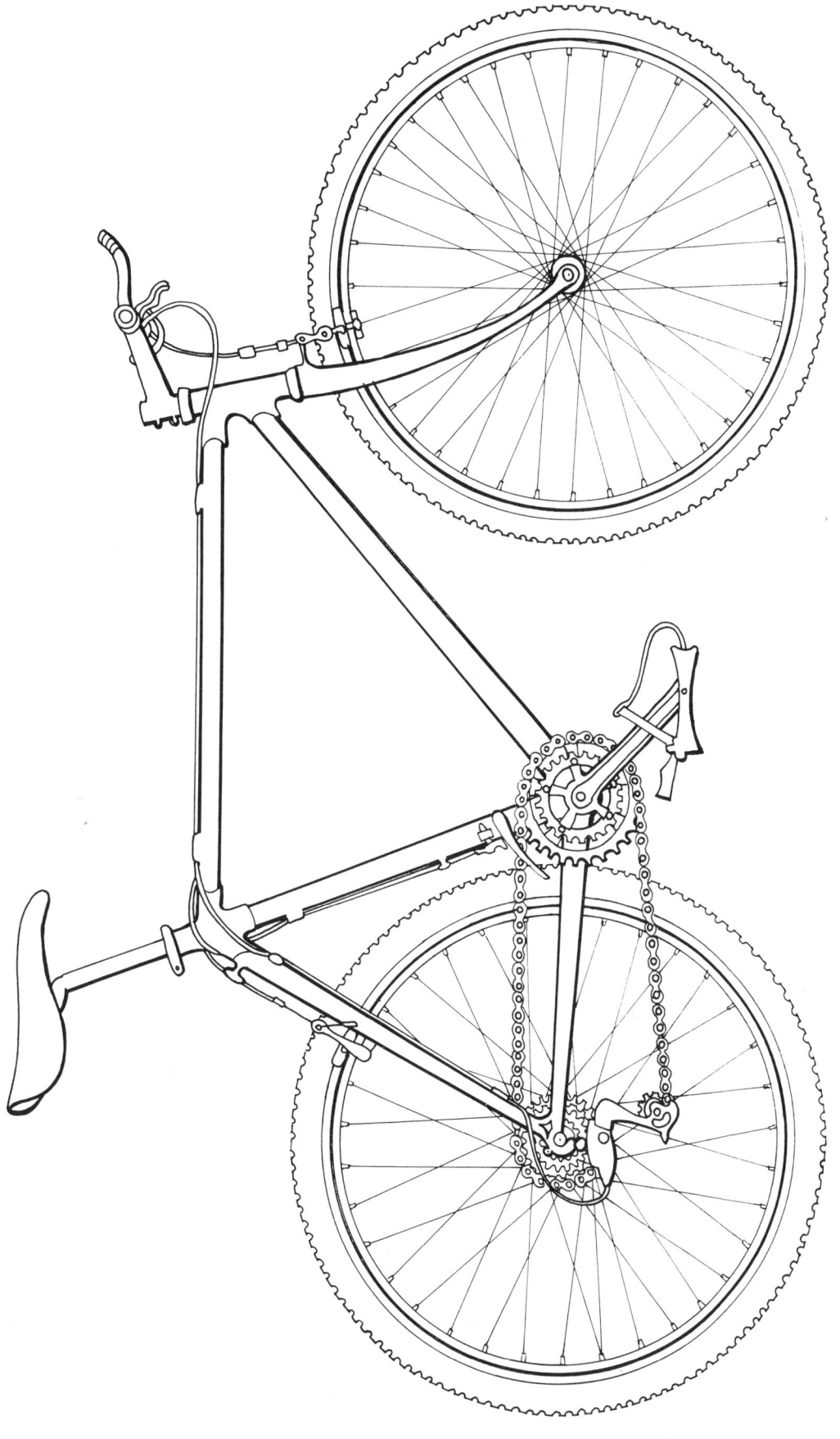

Copymaster 86

Name _____

Conservation/pollution

Suitable for all ATs

Copymaster 87

Name _____

Cooking

Suitable for all ATs

Copymaster 88

Name _____ Suitable for all ATs

Play safe

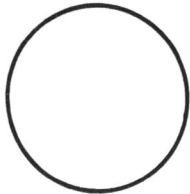

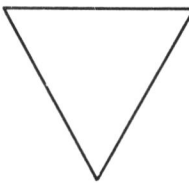

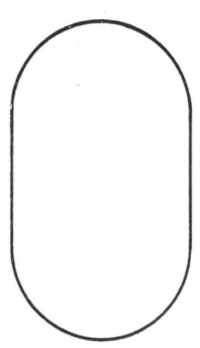

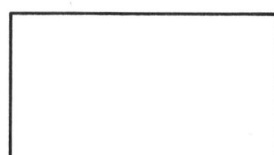 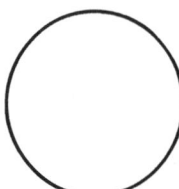  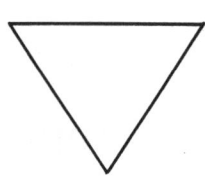

Name _____

PP

Weekend science: bottle band

Parents' point:
National Curriculum Science:
Physical processes.

Play a tune on some bottles.

You need: glass bottles and jars
water
two sticks.

To make: Arrange the bottles in a row.
Pour some water into each one. Play!

Try to find out whether differences in the shape of containers mean differences in sound. Is the amount of water put in important? Is the amount of 'space left' (air) in the bottle important? Can you arrange your bottles in order of pitch?

Introduction to sound production ✓
Tapping the bottles produces a vibration ✓

Name _____

Weekend science: shadows

Make animals and spooks on the wall.

Parents' point:
National Curriculum Science:
Physical processes.

Can you make a shadow duck, a shadow dragon, a bat or a bunch of flowers?

You need: a torch and a darkened room.

What you do: Rest the torch so that it shines on a wall. Move your hands and arms about to make all kinds of shapes. Look carefully.

Are shadows all absolutely black all over?

What happens if you move your hand nearer the wall? Nearer the light?

What else can you put in the path of the light to make a surprise shadow?

These four things make great shadows.

Light does not go through our hands ✓
When light is 'blocked' shadows are formed ✓
Shadows sometimes look less dark at the edges ✓

Copymaster 91

Name _____

M & P

Weekend science: dissolving

See what you can find that dissolves in water.

Parents' point:
National Curriculum Science:
Materials and their properties.

You need: large jug of water
see-through cup or glass
teaspoon
sink
rubbish bin
tea leaves, sugar, salt, etc.

What you do:
Half fill the glass with water from the jug.
Stir in one heaped teaspoon of one of the test materials.
Does it dissolve ('go into' the water)? Clean the glass. Dry the spoon. Try another material in fresh water.

Tick which dissolve in cold water.

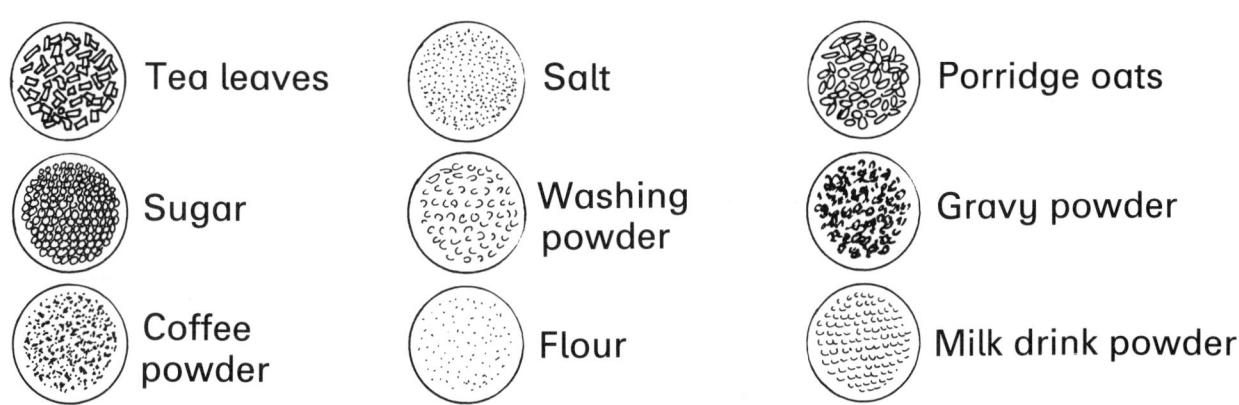

Now try again using warm water. Name the ones which dissolve in warm water.

Some materials are changed by dissolving ✓

Copymaster 92

Name _____

Weekend science: kaleidoscope

Parents' point:
National Curriculum Science:
Physical processes.

Make an infinite variety of beautiful patterns.

You need: three plane mirrors
glass beads
sticky tape
greaseproof paper
black paper
small torch.

To make: Stick mirrors together with reflective surfaces facing inwards. Stick greaseproof paper over one end. Stick black paper over other end. Make a hole in the black paper. Drop beads through the hole. Shine the torch on the greaseproof end.

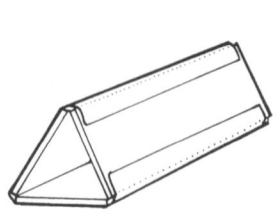
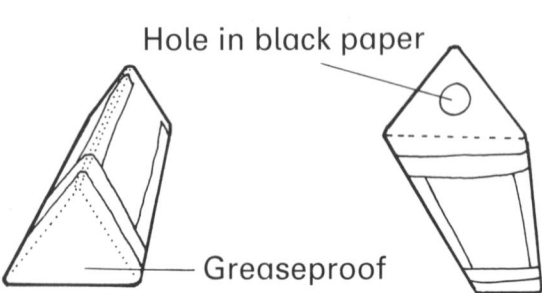

Hole in black paper

Greaseproof

| Light can be reflected repeatedly ✓ |
| We see when light strikes an object and some of this light is reflected into our eyes ✓ |

Copymaster 93

Name _____

Weekend science: periscope

Make light bend.

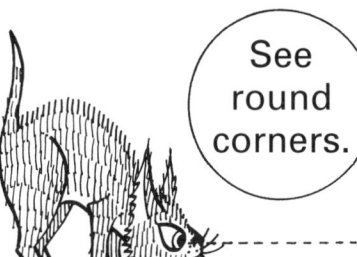

See round corners.

Parents' point:
National Curriculum Science:
Physical processes.

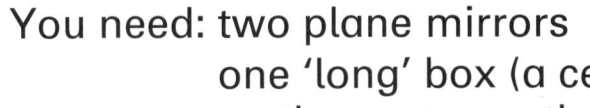

You need: two plane mirrors
one 'long' box (a cereal box cut up the centre so that the two halves can be pushed together is ideal)
ballpoint pen
scissors
ruler
protractor.

To make: Cut two pairs of matching slots at 45° on opposite sides of the box.
Cut a 'light in' panel and a 'viewing' panel.
Fix in mirrors so that reflective sides face one another.

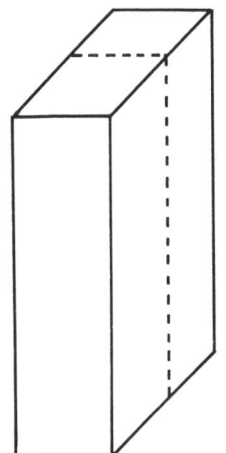 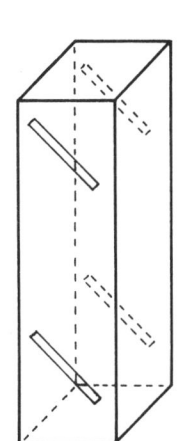 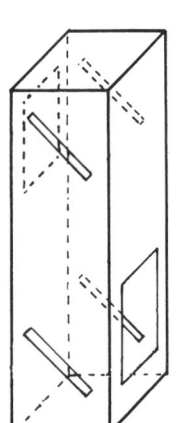 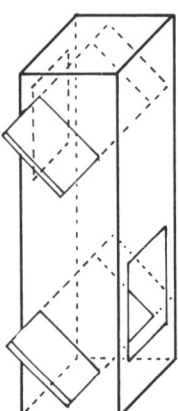

| Light travels in straight lines ✓ |
| Light can be reflected ✓ |
| We see when light strikes an object and some of this light is reflected into our eyes ✓ |

Copymaster 94

Name _____

Weekend science: marble timer

Make a marble run that takes exactly 30 seconds or a minute to complete.

Parents' point:
National Curriculum Science: Physical processes.

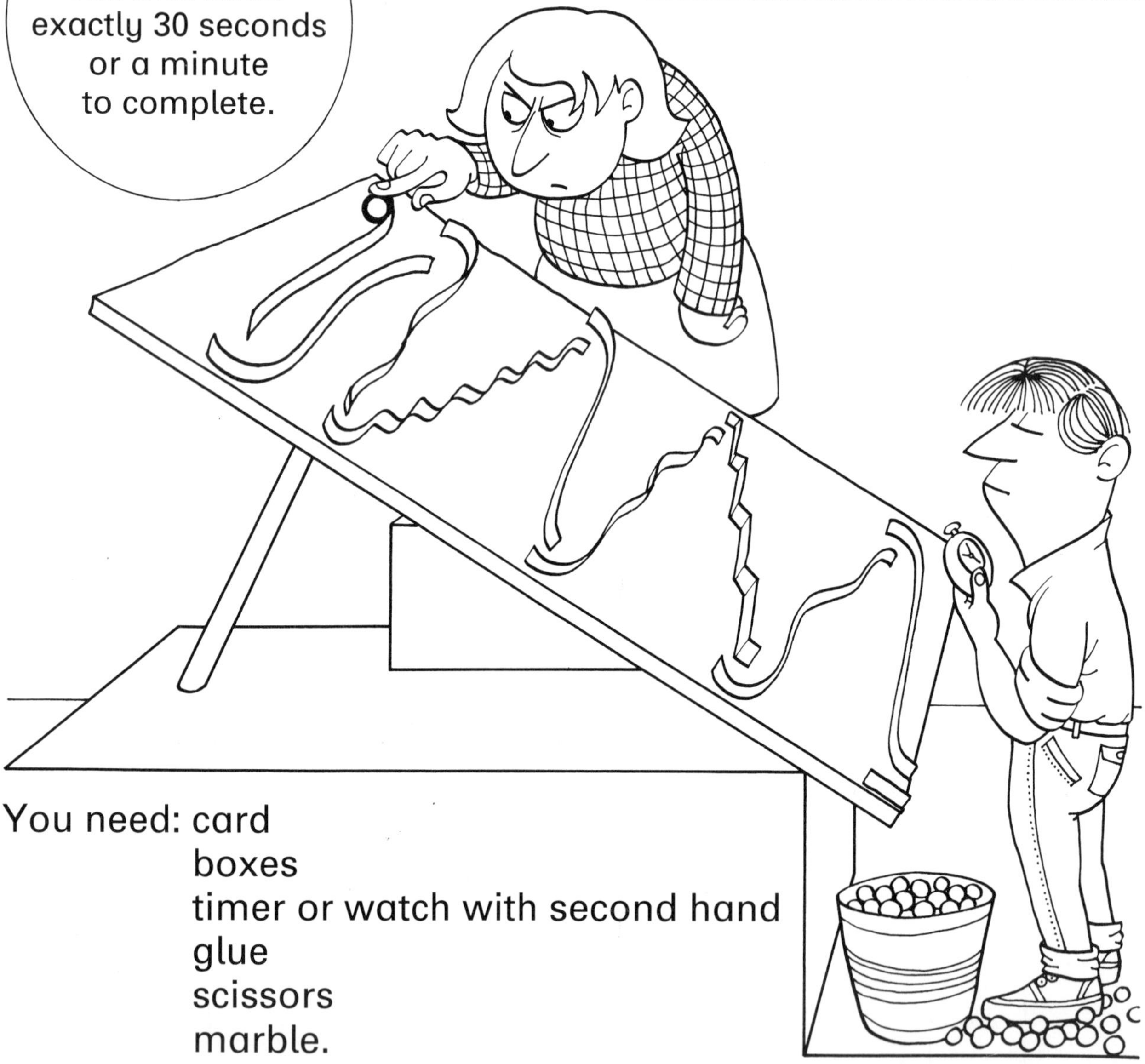

You need: card
boxes
timer or watch with second hand
glue
scissors
marble.

To make: Design and make some runs for a marble in a box or on card. Fix the runs so that the marble keeps going and does not 'escape'. If the marble comes through too quickly make its path more complex.

| There is a link between speed, distance and time ✓ |
| We can use gravitational force ✓ |